COUP
How America was Stolen in 2020

COUP

How America was Stolen in 2020

DRAKE ALEXANDER

ReadersMagnet, LLC

> "It's not who votes that counts.
> It's who counts the votes."
>
> *Joseph V. Stalin*

> "The struggle's no longer just who gets to vote.
> It's about who gets to count the vote."
>
> *Joseph R. Biden*

Dedicated to those in American gulags.

Coup: How America was Stolen in 2020
Copyright © 2022 by *Drake Alexander*

Published in the United States of America
ISBN   Paperback: 978-1-958030-54-7
ISBN   eBook: 978-1-958030-55-4

All rights reserved. No part of this publication may be reproduced, stored in a retrieval system or transmitted in any way by any means, electronic, mechanical, photocopy, recording or otherwise without the prior permission of the author except as provided by USA copyright law.

The opinions expressed by the author are not necessarily those of ReadersMagnet, LLC.

ReadersMagnet, LLC
10620 Treena Street, Suite 230 | San Diego, California, 92131 USA
1.619. 354. 2643 | www.readersmagnet.com

Book design copyright © 2022 by ReadersMagnet, LLC. All rights reserved.

Cover design by *Kent Gabutin*
Interior design by *Dorothy Lee*

TABLE OF CONTENTS

Preface 11
Chapter 1 13
Chapter 2 29
Chapter 3 39
Chapter 4 46
Chapter 5 57
Chapter 6 67
Chapter 7 79
Chapter 8 Part I 92
Chapter 8 Part II 102
Chapter 9 109
Chapter 10 Part I 123
Chapter 10 Part II 130
Chapter 11 135
Chapter 12 Part I 143
Chapter 12 Part II 152
Chapter 12 Part III 160
Chapter 13 168
Chapter 14 176
Chapter 15 184
Chapter 16 191
Coup Sources 200

PREFACE

This book has been written over the years from mid-2020 to early-2022. Most likely, new evidence related to the illegality, fraud, and irregularity of the U.S. presidential election of 2020 will surface during and after the time of this publication. Updated editions will be provided as new evidence surfaces over the years to come. But, in the meantime, is it not our duty and obligation to completely discover the mechanics of and work to correct this existential crisis? This outrage against our traditional way of life? This CRIME? In the words of Chris Hedges, a former correspondent for the *Christian Science Monitor*, National Public Radio, and the *New York Times*: "Either you taste, feel, and smell the intoxication of freedom and revolt or sink into the miasma of despair and apathy. Either you are a rebel or a slave."

"To be declared innocent in a country where the rule of law means nothing; where we have undergone a corporate coup; where the poor and working men and women are reduced to joblessness and hunger; where war, financial speculation and internal surveillance are the only real business of the state; where even *habeas corpus* no longer exists; where you, as a citizen, are nothing more than a commodity to corporate systems of power, one to be used and discarded, is to be complicit in this radical evil. To stand on the sidelines and say 'I am innocent' is to bear the mark of Cain; it is to do nothing to reach out and help the weak, the oppressed, and the suffering, to save the planet. To be innocent in times like these is to be a criminal."

CHAPTER 1

The 2016 presidential term of Donald J. Trump began with one of the biggest government fallacies since Saddam Hussein's "weapons of mass destruction" after special counsel Robert Mueller and his crack team of "patriots," along with America's top intelligence agencies, demonstrated one clear fact: the Russian government meddled in the 2016 presidential election. This was the first glimpse the public got of the Russian interference hoax.

In the summer of 2016, the stolen emails from the Hillary Clinton campaign and the Democratic National Committee were publicly released - some via the website WikiLeaks. Cyber security experts quickly suggested Russians were behind the hack; however, no evidence was provided to support the claim. Donald Trump routinely downplayed suggestions that Russia interfered during and after his campaign. As the run-up to election night continued in the fall of 2016, American intelligence officials briefed members of Congress that the Russian government was "looking to interfere" in the election. In September, at the G20 meeting in China, President Obama reportedly warned Russian President Vladimir Putin to stop his nation's interference in Western democracy.

Two months later, Donald Trump won the presidency, but before his inauguration, the Obama administration publicly pointed the finger at Russia for the Clinton email hack and, in retaliation, levied sanctions on Russia and expelled 35 Russian nationals from the U.S. The following month, a declassified intelligence report written with input from the FBI, the CIA, and the NSA stated that Vladimir Putin personally ordered a cyber and social media campaign to disrupt the 2016 U.S. presidential election - stating that Putin had a clear preference for Donald Trump. According to the report, Putin "aspired to help president-elect Trump's election chances, when possible, by discrediting Secretary Clinton and publicly contrasting her unfavorably to him." In February of 2018, Robert Mueller's first indictment against the Russians dropped.

The indictment charged 13 Russian nationals and three Russian companies for committing federal crimes while seeking to interfere in the U.S. political system. Mueller's team laid out a sweeping case directly accusing Russian citizens and companies of a massive coordinated disinformation campaign to sabotage the election. The defendants allegedly conducted what they called "information warfare" against the United States, with the stated goal of spreading distrust towards the candidates and the political system in general. The indictment accused the Russians who worked out of this building in Moscow of stealing American identities, setting up fake accounts on Facebook and other social media sites, and spreading false and inflammatory information. According to the indictment, their work isn't limited to the internet. Russians allegedly traveled across the U.S., hid their identities, and staged political rallies.

The Russians also had a favored candidate: "By early to mid-2016, defendants' operations included supporting the presidential campaign of then-candidate Donald J. Trump, and disparaging Hillary Clinton." Five months later, 12 more Russians were indicted by Mueller's team, including members of the GRU, a unit of Russian military intelligence.

They were accused of hacking and stealing the Democratic National Committee and Clinton campaign emails (it is important to remember that the Clinton emails showed Bernie Sanders being squashed by the DNC – Democrats cared less that they were caught, but more about who had revealed their bad behavior and who it benefited). After almost 4 years of this incessant investigation, none of the Mueller indictments indicated that any members of the Trump campaign were involved or aware of this meddling. If you recall back to the summer of 2020, I'm sure you'll remember a significant report talking about Russia, China, and Iran, all interfering in the 2020 presidential election.

In 2020, not surprisingly, the mainstream media claimed that Russia was the one assisting Trump, but the most novel addition was that outlets were then alleging that China and Iran were also intervening - but this time, to aid Joe Biden's efforts. The report came from the U.S. intelligence community, which was somewhat of a surprise given how the American intelligence agencies treated President Trump in 2016. There were countless anomalies surrounding the 2020 election between Joe Biden's senile rants, incoherent speeches, and the mail-in systems, which were universally problematic because of corrupt ballot counting conventions.

If you're an average American, you don't typically hear people talking about election meddling anymore. The 2016 fiasco went on for so long - I remember conversations regarding election meddling for the better part of two years, whether that be on the news, during interviews, or just discourse in the street - from when the investigations into Trump first began, shortly before the election happened, until the summer of 2019, during the Mueller testimony right after the counsel concluded and impeachment was declared. Once the Mueller report was publicized, the foreign interference topic quickly became tedious because it was so bogus and forced.

But just one year later, the details of the 2020 election woke the giant from his slumber, and now election interference has become one of the primary arguments for the Republican party. Back in mid-2020, the media commenced discussions regarding Kremlin-linked operatives attempting to boost President Donald Trump's candidacy, while claiming China wanted to see him defeated, according to the top U.S. counterintelligence officials. The report also read, "On Friday in a strikingly detailed update on American intelligence assessments about foreign preferences in the upcoming presidential election, Bill Evanina, a former FBI agent who was leading election security efforts at the office of the director of national intelligence, provided new information about what U.S. intelligence analysts have determined regarding the election interference goals of China, Russia, and Iran."

Evanina said the Russians, in a replay of the 2016 presidential election, were once again trying to help Trump by sabotaging his opponents. This individual said, "We assess that Russia is using a range of measures to primarily denigrate former Vice President Biden and what it sees as an anti-Russia establishment, that a pro-Russia Ukrainian parliamentarian is spreading claims about corruption, including publicizing leaked phone calls to undermine former Vice President Biden's candidacy and the Democratic Party." China, which intelligence officials say does not interfere as actively or as purposely as Russia, prefers President Trump, whom Beijing sees as unpredictable and unlikely to win re-election. Evanina said, "China has been expanding its influence efforts ahead of November 2020." He said they (China) seek to undermine U.S. democratic institutions and divide the country in advance of the 2020 election.

When I initially saw this report, I knew instantly that it was just more of the same old political marketing we'd seen for the past 4 years. I remember distinctly reading a very similar report during the democratic primaries: essentially a two-man sprint to the finish, between Biden and Bernie Sanders.

Conveniently, significant press coverage was released detailing a Russian conspiracy to help Bernie Sanders – coincidently right as Bernie was gaining momentum in the polls and directly after winning the Iowa caucus and New Hampshire. As soon as Joe Biden won South Carolina, the flood gates opened, accusing Bernie Sanders of winning because of "collusions with Russian hackers" and "Russian interference bolstering his numbers" – not because Sanders was promoting a populist message that appealed to young people and radicals. Of course not. No, it was due to Russian bureaucrats contracting hackers to one-up the establishment. Establishment losses are never a reflection of public opinion. That would be an absurd view. No, it was because Russia was simply cheating the democratic system, always conducting cyber-attacks and hacking state voting systems.

Suddenly, the media magically produced all of this "meticulous" information on Russian hacking campaigns when there was never any tangible evidence, but the theories put forth by these "experts" and the counterintelligence intel community officials were enough to convince the average listener that something was afoot.

The pattern became easily noticeable after 2016, which is why every time the odds were against the Dems, they conjured another falsehood. Those of us that looked for ourselves are yet to see a single Republican individual linked to the Russian government. The alleged "election hacking" was another white-lie written up in a staffroom of c-grade ABC writers, to further degrade President Trump and American democracy; the closest Russia came to "interference" were the several charges against 6 Russian corporations and 13 individuals.

The companies and individuals were unrelated to the Russian government. They ran pro-Trump Facebook ads in the Midwest, which constituted a very low-level campaign finance violation (non-citizens of the United States aren't permitted to buy political advertisements).

That was officially the closest American investigators ever came to any kind of concrete tangible evidence to 2016 Russian election interference. They amped up all of the "foreign interference in the election from Moscow and the Kremlin" rhetoric for years on end, and the best they could render from the entire years-long investigation were the 13 individuals who had nothing to do with the Russian government, individuals who set up a trivial social media ad campaign totaling somewhere in the five-figure range which, in the grand scheme of U.S. election campaigns, is minuscule. A serious campaign effort, taking Hillary Clinton by contrast, spent nearly a billion dollars in the 2016 election. Mueller got a handful of foreign nationals spending 5-figure sums on social media ads in the State of Michigan, and the media dubbed it collusion. Now, once again, in 2020, they were talking about Russia, but they were also talking about China and Iran.

What exactly were China and Iran doing, you ask? We're still not sure. This ceaseless plea to swallow their words opened my eyes to a vital revelation that many Americans should hear before they assume that elections have always been representative and unbiased. Our elections are influenced and interfered with every day by foreign regimes and civilians alike. It's no secret that the Democrats adamantly oppose Vladimir Putin's interference in the election, calling it a grave sin and a stain on the American people.

But even if that were happening, which it's not, it would be hypocritical to denounce foreign interference in one situation, but simultaneously openly welcome illegal immigrants to vote. When Russian nationals purchase Facebook advertisements, that's a crime, and if Trump did that, he'd be impeached without hesitation. If Trump colluded with any foreign nation, that would warrant impeachable actions. But then at the same time, we also saw sitting congressmen vouching for illegals at the border and aiding their efforts to unlawfully cross into California and Texas. Millions of Mexican nationals that walked across the southern border went on to vote in the 2016 and 2020 elections. Many of the 23 million illegal immigrants take advantage of the lack of election security and mail-in ballots.

Even if they're not, how many are participating in political rallies and protests? We know that many of them protest time and time again to defund ICE in the streets of the capital, in California (we saw them in 2016), and many other instances. So, God forbid the Russian government to interfere, but Mexico sends tens of millions of people, literally almost 1/10 of the U.S. population, migrating from Central America and Mexico into the United States.

But by the Democrat's standards, that's not considered interference. Then, of course, the elephant(s) in the room are all the countries that are permitted to interfere by law. Of course, it doesn't just stop and start at the immigrants that are interfering and that it is "permissible," but it's also foreign governments. The average voter might say, "That's not the same, that's immigrants. Completely different."

Well, what about Israel and Saudi Arabia, or what about Qatar? What about the number of countries that regularly interfere throughout the year? This isn't a secret. It's all public knowledge, yet it was simply glossed over during the Trump presidency. Last year, the Senate unanimously passed another foreign aid bill, greenlighting $3.3 billion annually for Israel, and at the same time, you've got an establishment PAC, where 2/3 of all U.S. congressman attend every single year, as well as sitting presidents and vice presidents, from both parties, all in attendance to listen to what the Arab donors and the Jewish donors have to say. The foreign aid money often reciprocates in the form of campaign and PAC donations. It is a tax-payer funded money laundering scheme to interfere with U.S. elections.

The listeners sit in on presentations from firms, all of which are only intended to buy voting power. But that kind of election interference is acceptable. Vladimir Putin, we simply cannot have that. Sheldon Adelson; however, that's totally fine. This brand of election meddling has been happening for centuries, since before Israel or the modern Arab gulf states even existed. Go back to Louis Brandeis on the Supreme Court, and his connection to the World Jewish Congress. It's not so much about election meddling because election meddling is pervasive across the entire country, so deeply rooted, and so influential when concerning immigrants or certain foreign governments. Aside from that, it has become such a nonsensical talking point now that sometimes when I hear about foreign interference, I think to myself, "does it even matter at this point?"

Let's say for the sake of the argument that Israel's interfering in the election, which they do. Mexicans are interfering in the election, which they do. Let's even say that Russia is interfering in the election, and China's interfering in the election; I'm thinking at this point, what difference does it really make? The point is we are not in control of our country, and we ultimately have no say over how these contests are decided. Do you know how much money it costs to run a presidential election?

Billions of dollars - and we're seriously supposed to believe that there is a significant distinction to be drawn between a foreign national who lives in Russia and a billionaire who lives in one of our coastal cities. We're supposed to believe that if Vladimir Putin or maybe even somebody that just lives in Moscow, meddles in the election, well, this is a violation of our sacrosanct democracy and they're going against our interests. You've got people that, in no meaningful way, are Americans who have residency and citizenship, that probably put up most of the money for the campaigns. This money in virtually every instance has "strings attached."

Most of the money stems from super PACs and non-profits, super donors, and mega-donors; these are people that do not live, talk or act anything like the common American citizen. The bureaucrats and lobbyists that live in Washington DC, Los Angeles, and New York City – they're post-national, or transnational, or anti-national because they see themselves as global citizens. They transcend American identity and many of them don't even have a primary residence because they also have a villa in the Cayman Islands, a summer home upstate, and another apartment in the city. They do not pay taxes. They do not go to the same schools. They have servants and private equity investments in adversarial nation-states. They welcome illegal immigrants and turn a blind eye when it comes to paying those illegal immigrants a living wage. It is all part of an oligarchical, elitist plan to create a feudalistic lord/serf society under the guise of "equity" or "anti-racism" or "compassion." To disagree is "racist."

We're supposed to believe there's a meaningful distinction; if you're a foreign national in Russia and you give money, that will be deemed subversive and not representative of the American people. However, you then have super donors like Sheldon Adelson or mega-donors like the Koch brothers with ungodly amounts of wealth, more than we'll ever see in our lifetimes, living in gated communities, jet-setting across the world, with the serfs to serve them. No doubt they're global citizens, but when they give millions and millions of their endless pots of money to super PACs, that's supposed to be more acceptable than a Russian Facebook ad campaign.

The people that are controlling and funding the elections, they're not normal – they're the aberration. The Democrats always like to play upon this patriotic theme of secure elections (only when it's convenient like when Russia's interfering in our elections). The Democrats and all the liberals, and the establishment alongside the deep state, suddenly become Bruce Springsteen or Clint Eastwood with flags waving and the national anthem on standby. Democrats like to pretend they're patriotic, and that's largely how they managed to prolong the Russia collusion throughout the Trump presidency.

The Manhattan liberals, or more broadly, the Coastal states, suddenly spring into life preaching all about American values, right up until they are burning flags when it's BLM (black lives matter) season. Nobody cared about America or the foreign sway over the elections when Portland or Minneapolis were burning.

The elite class does not care about America's interests or America itself. Most of them, for the most part, resent the American people. What made me chuckle was the thought that the people in Russia or China, as little as they may have, probably carry more appreciation for America than the people that are supposedly adamant patriots standing up against "foreign interference."

Take into consideration, this is all before we even factor in any of the institutions because, remember, we're strictly talking money here. In America, you can fund an election with $100 million when you're someone like Sheldon Adelson, but if you're a Russian national funding a Facebook ad with a 5-figure sum of money, there's no redemption for you; I feel I've said enough to make the point clear.

Money isn't the only factor when considering election results. What becomes of the American media? CNN, NBC, CBS, ABC, all these giant mainstream media conglomerates have more of an impact on how an election is won or lost than all the money from the 2 campaigns combined. Consider the overwhelming amount of institutional power the media has just by their market share alone. They also almost consistently contain the same scripted talking points, repeated over and over again until a lie becomes so pervasive that it is perceived as a truthful reality. Hunter Biden's laptop is Russian disinformation, Trump winning the 2016 election is Russian disinformation, Ukraine paid for Joe Biden's family's wealth – you guessed it, Russian disinformation. Pretty much, whenever they say the allegation is Russian disinformation, you can be sure it is true.

Then, take note of the stories they choose to cover and stories they choose not to cover. From late 2015 to the present day, can you even begin to quantify the value of the media's incessant anti-Trump coverage and how they were able to run interference for Joe Biden for the past 20 years?

It feels like 50 years since he became vice president and you think about all the terrible things Joe Biden has said and the bad policies he supported, or even solely on the premise that he's losing his mind. I do wonder, can anyone quantify, to the dollar, the value of all the negative press put out against President Trump?

That's just the news. You have 90% of all print media, and 99% of all television is liberal. Factor in social media giants like Google, Twitter, and Facebook suspending the Trump campaign on social media, hiding the President's tweets, and then completely banning him from all platforms, even going so far as to alter their algorithms and their terms of service to favor liberal users and restrict Republicans (shadow banning, throttling, search manipulation, etc.). Twitter continues to restrict major pro-Trump voices and their supporters. They also actively "reduced distribution" of the Hunter laptop story, claiming, wait for it - it was "Russian interference." This, of course, was a deceitful plot by the unholy alliance between intelligence bureaucracies, liberal pundits, and Big Tech.

Take into consideration the influence of transnational actors and the money they give. Quantify all of the media coverage and the social media bias. Quantify the unions and academia and throw all that in there for good measure, and the Democrats are paranoid and concerned that the Russians were hacking our election.

After a while, new actions don't matter anyway because, after a certain point, you have to realize that people lack agency, and it is simply a numbers game. The idea that we have 330 million Americans dutifully discerning and analyzing and making judicious decisions, voting free of any influence for that matter whether justified or not, in casting a vote is so ridiculous only children would believe it.

That every man, woman, and child in this country is dutifully going out to vote with no excessive influence on the part of any institution or foreign capital or foreign regime is absurd. We know by now that the way democracy works is that all the usual power players like the giant corporations, the media, the banks, the government, and Wall Street make the decisions. It's just a matter of pushing pawns around a chessboard; that's what democracy amounts to. The reason that they didn't like the Russian Federation interfering in the election was that the more a state like Russia interfered, the less influence that they have over their different pieces on the board, which thereby weakens their positions. All of these institutions are funded by foreign aid and told what to say and what to distribute; it's just about competition, and that's why I view Russia as a foreign actor in our election and no different than any of the major American institutions or entities, no different than any other foreign actor, of which there are hundreds if not thousands.

Russia has our interests at heart just as much as Wolf Blitzer and Jake Tapper, or CNN and Jeff Bezos and the Koch brothers, and anybody else in American politics who stands to further a corrupt agenda and hinder democracy. You hear the words out loud, and you almost refuse to believe this is where we are as a country. That a foreign government aligns with my interests no less than the foreign machine that's occupying our government, foraging and occupying every part of our country like we're all for purchase at some massive estate sale. The vultures will siphon off as much money as they can before the structure is condemned.

The end conclusion of this opening point is that the threat to our country and our democracy was never foreign interference. The biggest threat to our country is the deep state and the rise of this new neo-liberal, big-government big-business collusion, this "happytalistic" woke fascist state. The biggest threat to our country is the establishment - the transnational rootless ruling class that runs the country from the top of the pyramid because they are just as foreign as any foreign actors like Russia and China. The people that run the country are so foreign they might as well be a foreign regime, and we're living under their thumb.

They managed to completely overturn a presidential election, and the judicial system couldn't even stop them. That's the bottom line. In what meaningful way do you feel like the government represents you? In the last 20 years, did you ever feel like the government reflected your values and your lifestyle? This is an occupying regime, and they have well and truly buried themselves in our nest.

By now, I look at foreign interference from a completely different standpoint because the enemy doesn't come from outside our walls. It comes from within. What if Hungary, Poland, or Italy were interfering in our elections? Do you think they better represent you than the current administration? At this point, what do we do? A democratic election is supposed to reflect the voices of the people and in that process, the votes were cast and lies were proven. But because we now reside under the autarchy of this American empire, it seems that democracy has failed us, which is why I write this now. I'm not in favor of interference, but the media has disclosed on numerous occasions that Russia perceives the establishment Joe Biden represents as hostile to the people of Russia, and that's just the tip of the iceberg. In truth, the Biden regime that is in charge of our country is a danger to the entire planet. His cabinet comprises warmongers across the Middle East, in Russia, China, the Black Sea, and even South America.

The Trump administration was the only element of the American regime that represented the American people and their interests. It was the only office that displayed some semblance of realism, sanity, and humility when conducting foreign policy.

I look at foreign interference as virtually on par with everything else that goes on in modern America because when you break down Vladimir Putin, he reflects Western values more than our current government. If you listen to what he's said about Christianity, realism, and foreign policy, it's not that much different from many efforts made by past Republican administrations. He even reflects strong nationalistic impulse and a rejection of globalism which has plagued American governments for decades. Nothing makes this point clearer than the tragic invasion of Ukraine. While Putin is certainly a ruthless leader, he is vehemently, in his mind, protecting the interests of his people. Many in the Western world do not understand Putin's motivations for invading Ukraine. There is a strong historical context and connection between those two nations. Those that are condemning Putin were also the ones supporting the Iraq and Afghanistan invasions. Western democracies do not have the moral high ground that we often think we do, particularly since the year 2020, when censorship, political persecution, American gulags, compulsory medical mandates, the weaponization of the intelligence apparatus against the American people, and a two-tiered political justice system became "normalized." Disagree? Ask the truckers who in Canada were trampled, whose banks accounts were frozen, and whose rights were infringed by "Western democracy."

Compare a foreign country's views to our own government's and you start to see why this is such an issue. The truth of the matter about our country is that it's being ripped apart and picked apart from the inside. They draw up these arbitrary distinctions because it benefits them if Russia were to interfere in the looting, pillaging, and stripping apart of this country. It's not because the ballot is a sacrosanct patriotic expression. They hate this country. They hate the people in it. It's not about democracy or liberty. They just see Russia as another obstacle, and so they drop this pretext about "democracy versus Russia," but it's all just a façade, nothing more than a big excuse to carry on uninterrupted programming. Vladimir Putin is going to ruthlessly pursue the interests of Russia, but that cannot be said about our nation when democracy is overturned with the flick of a switch.

Just yesterday, as I write this now, Biden boasted of the might the U.S. military possesses and its nuclear cache, informing his citizens that if they try any sort of "rebellion" or "sedition," they'll lose. Twitter was quick to make light of the disturbing statement, but it once again proves just how little the current administration cares about the country. I also highly doubt that if 2 million armed citizens descended on the White House, there would be anything that could be done, or even if the military would be willing to do anything. But what an arrogant and un-American thing to say by Biden! If you do not reflect the will of the people, you have no authority to govern. That is basic.

Everybody, except for Donald Trump, and maybe a handful of others, have shown their gravitas in the wake of election results and vehemently rebelled against the outcome. Even with the astonishing compilations of evidence that have been racked up by patriots across the nation, the heat fizzled as the months rolled on, but in the last month, a spark of hope emerged from President Trump, calling on his supporters to not give in and to do whatever they can to bring the truth to light. I write this book as a window into the wrongdoings of those involved with the 2020 election scam, from President Biden at the top to the team of bureaucrats beneath him.

The book's goal is to provide a state-by-state dossier that will cover the major stolen states by the Biden administration and how the Democrats managed to steal the White House in plain sight. We are in a verbal civil war, and perhaps people around the fringes understand that America is now at a standstill. It is an ideological war of two opposing sides going beyond the constitution to bring order back to the United States of America.

We have heard elections have been stolen before. Bush stole it from Gore in Florida. Russia stole it from Clinton. But never have we seen, as a recent Times article put it, "a cabal of powerful people behind 'conspiracy,' 'shadow campaign' to shape the election." In other words, the 2020 election was not stolen by some distant foreign power or some meddling politician, but by a vast network of conspirators from Democratic governors who illegally changed voting laws to media companies that censored truth, and intelligence organizations that were weaponized against not only President Trump but the American people themselves. That is what makes 2020 an election year like no other, and this book will provide the methodical journey of what really happened.

CHAPTER 2

The mystery surrounding the 2020 election shaped the perspective of Trump voters for the rest of their lives. It was already suspected that intelligence agencies would target the Trump campaign in 2020 after it was discovered the FBI spied on the 2016 Trump campaign, using evidence assembled and deployed by the Clinton campaign.

Since then, half the nation understands the result to be the product of institutional deceptions on a mass scale. This propaganda was directed at the typical churchgoer, farmer, or blue-collar worker: the type who would gift their family members pocket constitutions for Christmas. The intel sector spying on a presidential campaign using fake evidence, including forged documents, was a great threat to their civil liberties because it meant nobody was safe. Trump supporters knew about the collusion hoax from back to front. They went from worrying the collusion was genuine, to questioning if it was legitimate, to realizing it was a complete con, and then watched as every institution berated them for years, just to pile on top of the already growing mound of falsehoods.

First, collusion was used to scare away decent people from helping the Trump administration during the campaign run and all his rallies across the nation. They knew their entire lives would be investigated if they cooperated with the Republican frontrunner, and they would face a lot of fees and legal action. Those who were brave enough to weather the storm were soon forced to quit because they were being bankrupted by legal fees. The Department of Justice, the media, and the government destroyed hundreds, if not thousands, of lives and actively subverted an elected administration based on a fallacy.

This is where the individuals whose political identity was largely characterized by a belief in what they learned in college began to see the outline of a regime that had crossed all institutional boundaries and stepped into margins unfamiliar to the modern West – only something you'd read about in a 20th century dystopian novel. That regime stepped out of the shadows to unite against an intruder amongst their ranks, a man they did not welcome with open arms - Donald Trump. A lot of Trump supporters understood this regime was not partisan. They knew that the same institutions would have taken opposite sides if it was a Tulsi Gabbard versus Jeb Bush election. It became increasingly difficult to describe to liberals how appalling and disillusioning the march became for conservatives, people who encouraged their children to enlist in the navy and chastise those who don't stand for the anthem. They could have handled the sense of betrayal if it solely stemmed from the government, but the behavior of the corporate press was what radicalized the masses on this issue. It wasn't only the political parties that lied to them, but the media, who by all accounts are described as impartial tellers of information and not propaganda machines.

They loathe journalists over the average politician or bureaucrat because they felt that the media had abandoned all reason. The idea that the press was driven by ratings and sensationalism became indefensible, if that were ever true, because they'd have been all over the Epstein story when it broke, but they weren't. The corporate press is the propaganda arm of the entrenched liberal bureaucracy and nothing anyone states will ever make them reverse that view. This was profoundly eye-opening and split the nation into those with eyes and those without.

Many Trump voters didn't know for certain whether ballots were faked in November 2020, but they knew with absolute certainty that the established order was now capable of telling a blatant lie and running free with it. They watched the press behave like beasts for an entire presidential election; tens of millions of people will always view Brett Kavanaugh as a serial rapist, based on a mass reported myth, because of networks like MSNBC and CNN. They would believe that the riots were "mostly peaceful" as cities behind them burned to the ground.

What's more is that they seemed proud of that outcome, as if they intended to drive certain individuals into the ground without an ounce of honor left for them to use in their defense. CNN even led a mob against a high school student and openly endorsed a summer of riots that led to billions in property damages and numerous deaths. Republicans always claimed the media had a liberal bias, but they still thought the press would admit the truth if they were cornered. Yet it seems this unveiling of the truth has only encouraged more companies to freely discuss their plans to sink American democracy and destroy the middle and working class. Let's look at a point made by Susan Molinari for example. She was a top lobbyist for Google and a senior executive at Google until 2018. She wasn't at the DNC to speak to anyone watching from home on TV, she was speaking to the Democratic Party itself.

Her message to them was very clear, "Silicon Valley is on your side and will help you win this thing.." By inviting Susan Molinari, Democrats also sent a message back to Silicon Valley, "You have nothing to fear from us and the Biden admin." Basically allowing them to retain their monopolies and openly inviting them to extend their control over America and the censoring of tens of millions of citizens.

This was a bargain a long time in the making. Immediately after Donald Trump was elected in 2016, executives at Google held a company-wide meeting; really, it was more of a group therapy session. The company's chief financial officer, Ruth Porat, broke down in tears as she spoke. She asked how Google could "use the great strength and resources and reach we have to continue to advance really important values."

What are those values? They're not conservative values. They are pro-globalist, pro-censorship, and authoritarian. The collusion between Big Tech and the Democratic Party is absolute and undeniable following 2016.

Google co-founder Sergey Brin was also devastated by Trump's victory; he found the election "deeply offensive." At the same meeting, he suggested Google change its algorithm, the core of the business, to promote a better quality of governance and decision making. In other words, they want to subvert democracy; everyone in the room knew exactly what he was saying, and they got to work doing it.

Two years later, a video of that company-wide meeting leaked; any other company would have been ashamed of it. The head of America's most powerful corporation, caught on camera, planning to manipulate voting in elections. But Google was not embarrassed. They didn't stop either; no one made them stop, so they continued.

Last year, a new video emerged. This video showed a woman called Jen Gennai, who works in the artificial intelligence unit at Google, confessing to trying to manipulate the 2020 election. Jen Gennai said, "We all got screwed over in 2016 so we're rapidly being like, what happened there and how do we prevent it from happening again?"

Once again, she's speaking about the results of a free and fair democratic election that Google, the most powerful company in the world, didn't like, so they're trying to make sure it never happens again - it's brazen. But they're doing it. Why are they doing it? What is there to gain?

Well, imagine you're them back in 2016, and you're a tech executive in Northern California. You're in your 30s, you're not particularly impressive though you have all the right credentials, and yet somehow you are now worth hundreds of billions of dollars.

You look on as Donald Trump wins the White House. He's running the most populist Republican platform since Teddy Roosevelt, and on the other side, openly socialist candidates are elected to Congress. People are tired of oligarchs like you. You have not improved America, so you know this could be very bad for you. Someone might tax your stock options or seize your private island. So, what do you do next?

Well, Silicon Valley had a few ideas. First, they boosted Democrats aligned with Wall Street and multi-billion dollar companies like theirs. As long as people were distracted by identity politics, as long as they were fighting about unresolved issues like race and gender, you might be able to distract them long enough then you could pull this off. You won't talk about the fact that you don't pay taxes if you're busy attacking cops and other powerless members of the working class.

So, there's a reason Kamala Harris and Joe Biden are now the standard-bearers of the Democratic Party. It's not because democratic voters love them so much. They didn't; it's because they're compliant. Joe Biden has trouble formulating sentences clearly; he's not posing a threat to tech monopolies, of course, especially not after 50 years of shilling for corporations, and no politician has demonstrated more clearly their ability to use racial tensions to divide the country more effectively than Kamala Harris.

Kamala Harris applauded the riots. She said: "That's right. For the first few weeks, but they're not - they're not gonna stop, and that they're not - this is a movement. I'm telling you, they're not going to stop before Election Day in November, and they're not going to stop after Election Day, and everyone should take note of that, on both levels, that this isn't going to let up, and the rioters aren't going to let up, and they should not."

This is the same Kamala Harris who stated that Michael Brown was murdered by cops in Ferguson. He wasn't murdered; that's not speculation. Barack Obama's own Justice Department concluded he wasn't murdered, but Harris repeated anyway, and her allies of Twitter allowed her to disseminate that line nationwide - they didn't pull that tweet down. So, Silicon Valley is doing all it can to help the Biden-Harris ticket, and this is just the beginning. Biden and Harris have consistently called Kyle Rittenhouse a racist murderer. No evidence was provided; no conviction was obtained. Those tweets remain online as of the writing of this book.

This year, for example, LinkedIn founder Reid Hoffman and other billionaires, through major financial support behind an organization called Acronym, reportedly set up bogus news sites in swing states to portray Democrats in a positive light, exactly like the propaganda they claimed Russia was propagating in the 2016 election.

Remember, this is the party that loves to complain about the death of local journalism, but they fund a propaganda network to change people's opinions before an election. The goal, of course, isn't just to make Democrats look good; it's to make you terrified because scared populations are easier to control. That's why Facebook blocked a video featuring the president pointing out an obvious scientific truth. No scientist disagrees with this. Children are mostly not at risk from the effects of the coronavirus. According to the scientific journal of The Lancet, the virus is generally a mild disease in children including infants.

Fatal outcomes are not just rare, they are nearly impossible. If you knew that, you might have real questions about the lockdowns Joe Biden, the teacher unions, and so many other institutions in this country are pushing to enforce.

So, you can't push it. Facebook decided you should not be able to see data from The Lancet. Twitter went a step further and had their 27-year-old liberal arts majors lockdown the president's campaign account until the campaign deleted the video themselves. In other words, Twitter told them to kiss the ring. They don't just erase the video. They need you to bow publicly to authority and do it yourself.

This has implications far beyond the election; far beyond who becomes president. This is about how much power the tech monopolies will have in future democracies and how much power that the professional class can continue to wield as the middle class continues to decay.

Technology executives in San Francisco are the product of those institutions, the left-wing universities. They've been trained to dislike the country that made their success possible, and they do anything they can to weaken social cohesion in this country or trust in our institutions. That includes pushing mail-in voting, which, as we know, abets voter fraud.

However, it's a very different story to watch the media invent stories out of thin air to destroy the livelihood of ordinary peoples' lives by sparking mass violence. Time Magazine said that during the 2020 riots, there were weekly conference calls, involving other leaders of the protest, the local officials who refused to stop them, and media people who frame them for political effect; in Ukraine, they deemed that type of action a color revolution, and for good reason.

During the singular summer of 2020, democratic governors took advantage of the coronavirus to change voting procedures. It wasn't just the mail-in ballots; they lowered signature matching standards and many other elements of the voting system to usher in new forms of voter fraud. It's also important to remember Hunter Biden's laptop. Big Tech ran a full-on censorship campaign against a major newspaper to protect a political candidate, even though if the roles were reversed, the story would have been plastered on every single major news network for the following 2 months. Even leftists couldn't refute that.

Every single tech corporation now admits it was a miscalculation, but the elections are over so what difference did it make? It goes without saying that if the New York Times had Don Jr.'s laptop, which is full of pictures of him smoking drugs and engaging in degenerate acts with lots of explicit emails describing direct corruption, the New York Times would not have been banned.

Think of the backstories about Trump being urinated on by Russian prostitutes and blackmailed by Putin were all endorsed as fact when the only evidence was a paper paid for by his opposition and disavowed by the very source that provided the intel. The New York Post was completely banned for reporting on domestic affairs for the same reason. The reaction of Republicans to all of this was not "no fair." That's how they reacted to Trump's "Grab them by the p***y" moment.

They wouldn't care about something so minor and somewhat trivial. This was different. Now they accurately witnessed that American institutions were owned by people who use any means to exclude them from the political process, and yet they still showed up in record numbers to vote in the 2020 election, despite the relentless attempts to demoralize the Republican base. Trump received 13 million more votes than his 2016 election - he beat Hillary Clinton's numbers by 10 million, and as election night progressed, his voters allowed themselves a moment of optimism that maybe their efforts were worth it, but when the 4 critical swing states, and only those 4, went dark at midnight, it was evident that something was amiss to all paying attention.

Over the ensuing weeks, they got shuffled around by grifters and media scam artists selling them conspiracy theories. They latched on to one another's increasingly absurd theories; they tried to put a concrete name on something very real. Media and tech did everything to make things worse. Everything about the election was strange, the illegal changes to election law, unprecedented mail-in voting, the delays, the blocking of poll monitors, voting machines connected to the internet, etc., but rather than admit that and make everything transparent, they banned discussion of it even in direct messages.

Everyone knows that just as Don Jr.'s laptop would have been the story of the century if everything about this election dispute were the same except the parties were reversed, suspicions about the outcome would have been taken very seriously. They understood why courts refused to take the election case. What judge would stick his neck out for Donald Trump knowing that he'll be destroyed in the media as a violent mob burns down his house?

It is a fact, according to Time magazine, that mass riots were planned in cities across the country if Trump won. Sure, they were protesting, but they were planned by the same people that did so during the summer. and everyone knows what that would have meant; judges have families as well. Forget the ballot conspiracies, it's a fact that governors used COVID to unconstitutionally alter election procedures, something that the constitutions of those states allow only legislators to do, to help Biden make up for a massive enthusiasm gap by gaming the mail-in ballot system.
They knew it was unconstitutional when they did it - it's right there in plain English in the many state constitutions. But they also knew the cases wouldn't be seen in the courts until after the election. What judge is going to toss millions of ballots because a governor broke the rules? The threat of mass riots wasn't implied, it was direct. Not every theory about election fraud is true, but Republicans are absolutely on the mark when they claim their

government is monopolized by a foreign regime that believes voters are beneath representation and will acknowledge no limits to prevent them from obtaining it. Are you still on the fence?

This book will bring to light some of the best evidence that 2020 was stolen from Republicans.

CHAPTER 3

As Election Day grew closer in 2020, Americans' suspicions grew, as Donald Trump and GOP representatives warned of the impending voter fraud caused by the flawed mail-in voting system. The plan to steal the election by hijacking ballot sites was on the mind of the average Republican, worried that their efforts were going to waste. But voting by mail has always been controversial in the eye of American politicians and weathered patriots. Absentee voting is a great system, but mail-in voting poses many concerns. Mail is lost all the time, so when mailmen indiscriminately transport millions and millions of ballots, it becomes very likely that the election numbers won't add up by the time they reach their destination. This way, you'll never know who won the election.

It is critically important to underscore how the media twists this story. You hear much of the time that no significant "voter fraud" was found in the election of 2020. That is, to some degree, accurate. However, they completely gloss over the real issue. What concerns most Republicans is not that there were widespread ballot "**frauds**" (traditionally meaning a forged ballot, but to be clear there was plenty of that, as well), but rather, **illegal** or **inaccurate** votes being counted (votes that never should have been counted or were counted incorrectly).

Most of you will probably think that voting by mail is a new concept, but it's not. It all started in what would become the United States of America; one of the earliest known instances of voting by mail was during the American Revolution. Yes, that's right.

In December 1775, a group of continental army soldiers couldn't make it back home to vote in Hollis, NH, so the town let the soldiers deliver their votes via a letter. Many soldiers also chose to vote by mail during the War of 1812. During that war, Pennsylvania let soldiers vote by mail if they were stationed more than two miles from their home, and that was even before trains. The first widespread use of voting by mail occurred during the American Civil War, as thousands of men remained deployed far from home in the build-up to the 1864 presidential election. To combat this, from 1862 to 1865, 20 northern states changed laws requiring in-person voting to allow deployed soldiers to vote. For the thousands of soldiers stationed far away from home, the states adopted their laws to permit them to vote using an absentee ballot, which led to controversy. Voting by mail stirred controversy among Americans when Civil War soldiers started filling out ballots from their military stations.

The problem quickly became partisan. As Republican candidates supported the cause and appealed to soldiers for their vote, Democrats feared that Republican military leadership would tamper with the results. An absentee ballot is valid, completed, and mailed in by a voter who couldn't physically be present in their home district on Election Day. Many of you have probably completed an absentee ballot the very first election you voted in if, perhaps, you were away at college in another district. Just a few years after the civil war ended, on the other side of the world, parts of Australia had begun experimenting with voting by mail.

By the close of the 1800s, many states had expanded their laws to allow homebound or traveling voters to participate in elections. Today, there are several anti-fraud protections built into mail-in balloting, including signature verification, drop boxes in secure locations, and address confirmation to make it harder for institutions and activists to hijack elections. By 1906, the whole country was letting certain citizens' ballots through the mail. But the difference is that Australia has a long history of being ahead of the curve when it comes to democracy. In the 19th century, in the United States, more and more states were passing laws to expand absentee voting to civilians.

In 1924, almost all the states had allowed at least a small demographic of their citizens to vote by mail in certain circumstances. This idea spread around the world to other countries that closely follow U.S. voting systems: Canada in 1917, West Germany in 1957, and Switzerland in 1970, among others. The Swiss liked mail-in voting so much that, today, the majority of Swiss vote by mail.

For the first time in 1991, any registered voter in Washington could apply, in writing, for status as an ongoing absentee voter. Using this option, ballots for every election are sent to the voter through the mail. In 1998, the U.S. State of Oregon became the first state to require all elections to be conducted by mail, though said voters still have the option to drop their ballots off at official drop sites. Since then, Oregon has saved a lot of money but has spent much more on-time tallying of the votes.

In 2002, several new laws were enacted in response to the close presidential election of 2000. States were required to replace punch card and lever voting machines, as well as the development of state-wide voter registration databases. Presently, Washington State, Colorado, Hawaii, and Utah also conduct their elections entirely by mail, and many other states also have counties and/or small elections where everyone votes by mail. Not only do they vote by mail, but today, dozens of countries around the world also allow mail-in voting. Even though it has happened in so many places, and it's been around for such a long time, it's still controversial.

It has been controversial ever since it was first widespread back during the civil war. During the civil war, it almost immediately became partisan. Republicans viewed a higher voter turnout to help them get elected, so they tended to support mail-in voting, while Democrats felt mail-in voting could hurt their chances of winning elections, so they opposed it, and fought it in the courts. Ultimately, four states got rid of mail-in voting because of this. There are numerous potential problems with mail-in voting, which is why it becomes such a hot talking point during elections.

1. The tallying process is incredibly long and tedious.
2. A ballot could get lost or stolen in the mail or not processed on time.
3. A voter request could be altered or forged to suit a certain candidate.
4. A voter can be more easily swayed by family members or caregivers to vote a certain way or paid to change their vote at the last minute.
5. Mail-in votes are **unsolicited** (remember these are different than applied-for absentee ballots), meaning individuals can vote multiple times through different means. Lost mail-in ballots can simply be filled in multiple times by the same or imaginary individuals when relaxed integrity protocols are the norm. This is also ripe for ballot harvesting which is illegal in most states.
6. Sabotage - anybody could intercept ballots in the mail and tamper with them, even the postal workers themselves.
7. Forgery - many ballots contained no required signatures, and ballots can be forged with very little skill or resources given a lack of meaningful oversight.

8. Corruption - people who count the votes are easily given too much freedom when it comes to rejecting ballots, or bias in those same folks could simply ignore or falsify ballots. This can quickly be changed with a sneaky bribe or propaganda tool.
9. Adjudication - Most states use electronic scanning equipment to read mail-in ballots. These machines are prone to error and "adjudicators" have the power to change your intended vote on their own, without your knowledge or consent.

That's just the tip of the iceberg. There are many more potential problems that we'll cover state-by-state. We shouldn't be entirely biased, though. The history of mail-in voting doesn't mean that voter fraud can't potentially happen with other citizens voting using paper ballots or through electronic means. However, the unsolicited nature and weak security measures make mass mail-in voting extremely prone to illegal and inaccurate vote tallying. Even minor errors of, say, half of 1% can lead to tremendous consequences for the representative nature of a democracy.

While paper ballots are still considered more secure than online voting, most places will have to deal with counting paper ballots. Even with voting in person, ballots are lost or stolen, and the people who count the votes have the chance to tamper with the results, or at the very least, impose some underlying bias to change the tide. Most of the potential problems with mail-in voting I previously mentioned could simply be resolved with tightened security measures, but as we have seen over the past few years, security measures can easily be infiltrated when you have the appropriate infrastructure, namely Democrat governors that change the integrity rules unilaterally without legislative authority.

According to a study by The Washington Post, there is "no evidence" that mail-in voting increases voting fraud, so we can rest easy knowing that Jeff Bezos' blog has ratified the election integrity for us. In the presidential election of 2016, 33 million Americans voted by mail. A total of 24% of all Americans voted in the election. That is a staggering number. Remember, there is a difference between fraudulent and illegal votes.

President Donald Trump took great interest in the election and went on to appoint a Commission to oversee the election and inspect whether voter fraud was committed on a mass scale because he knew that millions could easily vote illegally when basic lawful practices are breached by corrupt politicians and officials. As Trump won the 2016 election, the Commission naturally found little evidence of voter fraud, though it was apparent that those niche areas were being exploited on a minute scale.

Still, for the upcoming 2020 election, Trump made it his mission to undermine mail-in voting to cancel out those voting systems and turn people away from the controversial practice. It's no secret that mail-in voting has quickly turned into a political issue.

The average voter probably wonders how an issue as banal as the Postal Service can be so political, but the unfortunate truth is that it hasn't only been politicized for the sole purpose of elections. From highways and railroads, fostering industries like telegraphs, cars, and airlines - it even had a hand in the early development of the internet. Yet it's also been a way for politicians to give kickbacks to their cronies, breaking down free speech and pushing unsuccessful economic policies through conniving means.

The U.S. postal system has both been used and abused by politicians throughout its history, which is why Trump has been so bullish on this issue since his election. After the witch hunts found nothing to convict Trump, the last tool the Democrats had up their sleeve was voter fraud.

Due to the nature of America regarding the COVID pandemic, voting by mail dramatically expanded nearly everywhere in the country, leading to a huge spike in illegal votes. In the face of the coronavirus pandemic, voters in every state but Mississippi and Texas were allowed to vote by mail or by absentee ballot in last year's primaries. It is important to stress that in many of the states that expanded mail-in voting, Democrat governors changed the requirements of those ballots illegally by removing signature requirements, postmarks, and identifying information, all items that have nothing to do with COVID or the safety of voting. What does requiring you to mail your ballot in by Election Day have to do with the safety of the voter?

Around 84% of Americans were allowed to mail in their vote for the 2020 election, leaving many wondering how many methods the Democrats employed to achieve such an outcome using the absentee ballots. According to post-election polls, one out of three Americans voted using their mail-in privilege. For those Americans who voted by mail for the first time in the 2020 election, know that **most** of your ballots were safely accounted for, but not **all** were accounted for up to par. And when you are dealing with tens of millions of ballots, and the election was determined by 10,000 votes here, 10,000 there, even small margins of error can have dramatic consequences.

CHAPTER 4

Election night 2020 was a blur for many, as they watched the immense lead Trump gained throughout the evening shatter in less than an hour. So, for the sake of everyone who can't quite remember exactly how it went, let me take you back to that November, and how the electoral proceedings played out in real-time. For most of you, winning the election was in sight, but as November passed and December flew by, it became a running joke as to how long-winded the process had become. Before we look at how the evening concluded, it's imperative to know which states were going to be strong indicators of the outcome, and which states took the longest to reveal their count. So, let's run through some of the swing states, in no particular order:
- Pennsylvania
- North Carolina
- Georgia
- Michigan
- Wisconsin
- Nevada
- Arizona

At least 3 to 4 of these states were of vital importance to the Trump campaign. I say that because President Trump had a hard time reaching the 270 electoral votes he needed without winning certain states, according to the polling at the time, and because of just how delicate the election was once those swing states started announcing votes. Not to mention, these were states that served as strong indicators of the outcome.

The two most important states during the election were Florida and Pennsylvania, primarily because Donald Trump had a tough road to 270 without at least one or the other, and if Biden won both, then there was probably a good possibility that he would win the election overall. In either case, these two states represented a crucial 49 votes, which in retrospect, would have determined the winner of the election. Ohio was another state to watch, especially given its history.

It's certainly worth noting here that no Republican has ever won the White House without Ohio, and it has consistently voted for the winner of every presidential election since 1960. So has Florida except for 1992, so not only did Ohio and Florida carry big electoral vote numbers, but they also served as bellwether states that indicated the direction of the election. One thing we need to point out about some of the swing states we've just mentioned: in states like Texas and Arizona, changing demographics have trended them from more solidly red states into purple swing states. That said, if either state goes blue, it would be a signal of that shift getting stronger for years to come. It's also worth noting here, but it was entirely possible, not to mention quite likely, that voters wouldn't know the winner on election night due to a multitude of mail-in ballots which were expected to be returned on, or after Election Day. However, different states had different rules for counting ballots, as numerous states experienced trickled results when votes are counted day-to-day or every other day.

In the same vein, election results are typically delayed if the margins are very close, giving credence to the voter fraud motive, given that Biden was losing badly throughout the evening. In Florida, for example, according to Ballotpedia, a machine recount occurs when the margin is less than or equal to 0.5% of total votes for the office. Rules do vary from state to state, but we'll get into that when we break down the results state-by-state. If the results are close voters typically find themselves waiting even longer. Another factor to note on election night, believe it or not, is the weather forecast.

I say this for two reasons - firstly we know the weather on Election Day was mild and rather banal, nothing out of the ordinary for the majority of states. This is mentioned because weather patterns can influence whether people go out to vote, but it could also affect the mood of voters. A study conducted in 2017, by 3 professors at the University of Chicago, Pittsburgh, and California, found Democrats were more likely to stay home during poor weather, thus benefiting the Republican candidate.

They surmised that the weather could have played a part in both the razor-thin elections of 1960 and 2000, and we do know that weather events can affect an election, such as Hurricane Sandy that hit the East Coast just days before the 2012 election, in which then-President Obama infamously hugged the then-governor of New Jersey, Republican Chris Christie. However, it likely never made a difference in the 2020 election given the high volume of mail-in ballots that were dispatched; something else to be watching at exit polls, but as I just discussed, exit polling didn't make as much difference this time due to the wide influx of mail-in voting. Mail-in ballots have never been used to such an extent in U.S. elections before, so there was always going to be trouble and ways to infiltrate this exposed system. We can almost certainly count on a pundit to make prognostications and accusations of voter fraud.

Let's start with prognostications when pundits and news organizations make predictions about who is likely to win a state on election night. When you hear newscasters calling a state for a candidate, that's exactly what they're doing, predicting a winner, and they're very often right in these prognostications, but when they say that North Carolina has gone to X, they're making a prediction based on polling demographics. Essentially, they make the call when one candidate is sufficiently far ahead that it is unlikely their opponent could catch up. This gives the appearance that on election night, we normally know the results, but even in a normal election, this has never been true. Even in normal elections, it takes time to process all the ballots. After all, even states which don't normally offer extensive mail-in voting still have to accept ballots from military personnel abroad and citizens living outside the country. This system always causes a delay; therefore, election night has never truly been "one night." 2020 was even longer, though, due to increased mail-in turnout. However, that's not nearly sufficient evidence to accuse parties of malfeasance. These votes are usually just as valid (but not always) as any other, so for them to be ignored or left uncounted would be a serious democratic issue.

Just because pundits or news organizations call a state doesn't necessarily mean it's all over, it never does. But in 2020, it's especially true as the count was still ongoing. Even in a normal year, you should expect these state calls to come a few days after. As you might normally expect, people don't like mentioning the painful experience that was the election of 2000, but it's perhaps the obvious choice when it comes to talking about the dangers of prognosticating in democratic elections. In 2000, news outlets began calling Florida for then-Democratic Vice President Al Gore, only to retract later in the evening and then call it for the Republican Governor of Texas George W. Bush. When Gore retracted his concession phone call, it began a month-long electoral crisis, in which Americans had to wait for lawyers and politicians to come to terms. In the end, the issue ended up before the U.S. Supreme Court.

I won't bore you with the details of the hanging chads or the recounts that occurred. Suffice to say that the ruling in favor of Governor Bush ultimately handed him the victory. I say all of that because elections are unpredictable until the very last counties disclose their votes. Ordinarily, media outlets can predict the outcome early, even though counts continue for days to come. In 2020, the counts took weeks, most certainly an aberration in U.S. elections. My advice would be to take any prognosticating with a grain of salt; with the massive amount of mail-in voting, it was always guaranteed that there would be claims of voter fraud from either side. And as predicted, the issue ended up in court. Let's look at how the end of the election played out in real-time.

Here's the map coming out of election night. As things stand the morning after the election, this wasn't the result that many Democrats were hoping for. But despite Trump's comments, "this isn't over just yet.." As you can see, there are still battleground states where votes are being counted, and therefore, things could change. So, let's run through the battleground states, starting with the ones that have already been called. Before moving on to those where we had fewer results at this point, let's start with Florida because, ultimately, that's where the night started, and that's because Florida was quick to report its figures on election night. Those results told us that President Trump retained the state with a decisive victory, at least by Florida standards. Although polling on Election Day for the state was close and well within the margin of error, Biden did have a lead of a couple of points, making Trump's victory of a few points quite surprising. His vote share in the state was the highest we've seen since 2004, for George W. Bush.

Ultimately, some attribute this result to Miami, Dade County, usually a democratic stronghold where votes can be accumulated in large numbers. Trump's share of the vote drastically increased in this county, and while not winning, his increased support significantly cut into democratic support in the state as a whole. This shift towards Trump can be put down to a large surge of support from certain Latino groups, specifically Cuban Americans, who tend to vote for Republicans as a result of the historic issues with Cuba under Fidel Castro's socialist government. Without Florida, Trump's path to the White House would have been incredibly difficult, so it was a great start to his election bid. Despite speculation in the days running up to the election that Texas could swing for Biden, President Trump managed to win the state and crush democratic dreams of a more purple Texas in 2020, with over 50% of the electorate in favor of re-electing the president. This was a significant event, as Texas is allocated a whopping 38 votes in the Electoral College. At the beginning of the count, it did look as though Biden would win the state. However, as more votes were counted, it became clear that this was not the case. The turning point was around the 50% mark when Trump overtook Biden.

This means that if Biden wants to win, he'll have to look elsewhere for the numbers to get him across the 270-victory line. Like in 2016, Ohio was a decisive victory for President Trump. At an early stage in the night, it looks as though there could be a major upset on the cards with Vice President Biden's votes surging in comparison to Trump's. However, this proved to be the illusion that many expected, as the early vote and promptly counted mail-in ballots in the state were heavily in favor of Biden. That was until Election Day votes were counted, and the picture moved quickly towards the GOP. Remember, Ohio is also a key bellwether state in the U.S., having voted the same way as the presidency since 1964, so we have to see whether they are just as right this time around. Iowa, in a similar way to how it played in 2016, went decisively to President Trump; with 99% reporting, Trump won an 8-point victory. This is down from the 9.4-point win in 2016 but remains indicative of Trump's support among white working-class voters in parts of the Midwest and the central United States.

While this isn't a surprising result, the size of the margin between candidates may shock people, as polls were consistently predicting a much closer race. For the first time in 24 years, it looks like the Sun Belt state of Arizona may have gone to the Democrats. President Trump won the race comfortably in 2016 over Hillary Clinton - following the loss of Florida, this was an important, though not essential, state for Biden to pick up, so his team would certainly be happy with this result. Analysts feel that the growing young Latino population in the state helped push the Democrats over the edge. It wasn't just Biden who had success on election night though, with democratic Senate candidate Mark Kelly unseating his Republican opponent. The Democratic Party will be looking to consolidate Arizona over the next four years and turn it into a solidly blue state, and they'll also be hoping that shifting demographics across the country could cause a similar change in other states as well. Minnesota has gone decisively to Vice President Biden. It wasn't expected to be the closest of battleground states, with a 538 polling average, giving Biden a major lead on the eve of the election.

However, because Hillary Clinton only won the state by 1.5 points in 2016, it was worth keeping an eye on. And for 2020, the results were much more emphatic, with Biden winning well over 50% of the vote, putting to bed any democratic nightmares in the state. None of the major networks have called the State of Georgia. It's currently quite tight, although President Trump does have a slight lead in the ordinarily red state. I say ordinarily because Georgia has been a state in the campaign that the Democrats have had their eye on, with the hope of potentially flipping it. While all signs point towards an unsuccessful democratic night in Georgia, and the final result should go in Trump's favor, we cannot at this stage give a decisive decision because some of the areas still to declare votes are in more democratic leading counties. So, Biden could still pick up a good number of votes. North Carolina is in a similar situation to Georgia; no major network has called the result, and the current numbers show the race within a couple of points but leaning in the president's favor. North Carolina was predicted to be one of the key states that, if lost by Trump, dramatically narrowed his path to 270. It is slightly too close to call right now, and the situation could change. Pennsylvania is a bit of a mess results-wise at the moment. Election Day voting made up the majority of the reported results, which as expected, gave President Trump a handy lead. There are still masses of votes to count and reports, including over a million mail-in ballots, which are expected to shift the results toward Biden. Statistics are ever-changing. In the run-up to the election, Nevada has consistently been assigned as a blue state after Clinton won it by 2.5 points in 2016, with not much credence being given to the fact that it was a potential Trump pick-up. There is still a way to go, and it's still too close to call. Biden currently has a razor-thin lead, but the Democrats haven't done as well as expected or even as well as they normally do, especially in Clark County, where Democrats normally pile up the votes.

As in every state, there are still some mail-in ballots to count, but in Nevada, they're allowed to be received up until the 10th of November as long as they are postmarked by the election date, a standard rule for the state. The secretary of state warned that there won't be another update until Thursday, saying they're focusing on mail-in votes, which could mean the upcoming votes will favor the Democrats.

This is proving to be one of the more confusing races of the night, and it's impossible to call, but if Biden loses Nevada, it looks increasingly unlikely for him to be able to claw the election back. Wisconsin is looking very important for Biden, and it's incredibly close. Biden still has a tight lead in Wisconsin, but as said, it's unbelievably close. Democrats were hoping that Biden would be able to pull ahead following announcements from Milwaukee, but with essentially all the Milwaukee votes announced and the margins still pretty small, it's looking worrying for Biden. It seems the majority of these votes are mail-in, which might help Biden, but the votes represent counties that lean Trump so they might help him instead.

Trump is ahead in Michigan, but it seems that this is a case of a red mirage, due to skewed Election Day voting, in favor of the Republicans. This isn't saying Trump can't win, but there is a big expectation that mail-in ballots being counted after the polls closed could massively shift the vote in Biden's direction.

This is primarily the case in Wayne County, the most populous county and home of Detroit, which alone could change the course of the whole election. The Michigan secretary of state thinks they'll probably have the result by the end of the day. What can be said for certain, is that Michigan will be a lot closer in the end compared to how it looked throughout the night. So, while some of the swing states have already been called, the race simply isn't over.

There are still certain key states yet to be called, and depending on which way they fall, could lead to a Biden or Trump victory. Ultimately, voters have to wait and see which way these states fall. In his remarks on the night, Trump commented on the delay, stating: "All of a sudden, everything just stopped. This is a fraud on the American public. This is an embarrassment to our country. We were getting ready to win this election – frankly, we did win this election. For the good of this nation, this is a very big moment. This is a major fraud in our nation."

Trump seemed to have expected election results to be called on election night, as did millions of voters watching the states input their numbers throughout the night, but that simply did not happen. COVID, mail-in ballots, early voting, and the fact that some states were still counting allowed for many states to withhold their results and alter the numbers. **The legitimacy of these unprecedented actions forms the crux of tens of millions** of Americans distrusting the 2020 election. Were those activities legal? Prudent? Accurate?

Around 11:25 Eastern time on Saturday, CNN and all other outlets projected Joe Biden to have won the State of Pennsylvania, taking him over the required 270 electoral votes and thus giving him the presidency. While counting continued in many states, the networks saw enough to make the call that everyone had been waiting for since Tuesday night.

This certainly wasn't the end of the road for the election drama as the Trump campaign prepared and, in some cases, already put forward election fraud lawsuits, as predicted. But during this stage, the majority of these claims seem to be without a great deal of evidence and were merely speculation. Voters knew something was suspicious, but at the time they couldn't identify what. The strange suspension of election counting in several key states (all of which occurred virtually simultaneously and all of which ultimately went to Biden by a razor-thin margin) left many people simply with the thought that something was wrong with this election. However, unless something drastic changed, the media and, more importantly, the new president and vice president were beginning the transition into a new era - perhaps illegitimately so.

The hard-hitting election result was centered around Pennsylvania, as anyone who's listened to a Biden mumbling speech too many times can tell you that Pennsylvania was the president's childhood home. The political and emotional center of the year and its additional position as a swing state elevated it to a strange position in America, and for a brief moment, it looked like Trump might win the coveted state. But of course, he didn't, and as made clear in recent chapters, it all came down to voter infiltration and malfeasance.

And with the final vote swinging Pennsylvania back to Biden, America's scariest trio of swing states was now once again backing the same candidate, but unlike in 2016, Michigan, Wisconsin, and

Pennsylvania pushed the Democrats over the edge. To complete the symbolic circle, Donald Trump was playing golf when he learned he had lost the election. Unbeknownst to his cabinet and advisors, the Democratic campaign wasn't as covert as they thought they were when stealing the election, and just 2 months later, the truth started to leak out from the seams.

CHAPTER 5

As the months rolled on after November 2020, numerous documents and sources have been released displaying clear anomalies regarding election integrity. It was no secret that Trump was skeptical as to whether or not he'd win the election on paper given the wide range of systems that the Dems would be able to use to their advantage. But some of the most notable, and perhaps the best, indicators that the election was fraudulent were the figures released by precincts that partook in the election. First, we need to cover a basic concept that everyone should need to familiarise themselves with before trying to read the figures and graphs. Fundamentally, think about a mailbox as your voting system, where just like any system, there's an input for each person to post their letters and an output for the postman to then deliver those letters.

This is a very rudimentary model, and just like any system of this simplicity, both the input and the output should be unambiguous and easily trackable so that regulators can trace in a very clear way. Evidence in the majority of cases will be essentially explicit.

What most Americans realized in 2020 was those very systems, such as input door voting systems, don't have voter registration cards - Americans don't have authentication; receipts directly given to the person who voted are not commonplace, so citizens struggle to prove who came into that precinct and cast their decision.

In short, there's no definitive proof of your voting, so the input has some issues. The additional element is the output. For example, if we're assuming the output reflects what took place in the election, consider an input with 30 votes was registered, 10 voted for Candidate A, and 20 voted for Candidate B; the output should be 30 ballots in total.

All of this is factual under the governing principle that the system CANNOT change the output. Now, if that were possible, and the system could alter the output, then uncertainty becomes the primary concern of the result since the output can be manipulated. Simply put, the inputs are clear-cut, and the outputs can be manipulated.

Election integrity is what all patriots want – to uphold democracy and defend the votes of citizens.

Ultimately, ballots are either hand-counted, with people thoroughly reviewing the ballot authenticity and looking for your hand-counted ballot, or they can be machine-counted where processors convert your ballot in a machine and transfer the count into an image, which is called a ballot image.

Those ballot images are then tabulated. Machine-counted valid images are not trivial in the democratic realm. They are a vital process of the counting procedure. The problem Republicans are facing in many states is that officials failed to save their ballot images. This incident led to pending lawsuits, forcing the state and numerous counties to preserve those ballot images as valid evidence.

Unfortunately, for the majority of the population, the ballot images were destroyed. What many analysts noticed in Massachusetts was a trend of some serious irregularities regarding ballot images whereby the ballots were destroyed or deleted during the election process. This major anomaly was the catalyst for a nationwide investigation into swing state counties. Following the discovery, Massachusetts claimed their state passed a statute, one that allows the state to destroy ballot images.

This statute was never cited or referenced in any lawful way, which was a clear violation of federal law. Former federal candidates noted that states must save the ballots for 22 months following an election, professing that all records generated in connection with a particular federal election must be digitally stored for federal archives. This practice was rampant across the country during the 2020 election.

As an election official, if you're using the ballot images to count the votes, and other officials questioned the count without the ballot images, the election process is null and void unless they allow officials to hand-count, which is an extremely tiresome and complex job. A primary feature in the voting system called Weighted Race Feature, dating back to 2001 as far as we know, specified in the manual, and well documented, allows the system to tally by weight. For example, if Candidate A receives 1000 votes, and Candidate B received 1000 votes, the current system can weigh Candidate B's votes to where his/her votes would register 2:1, giving him/her two votes for every single vote processed, and also halving Candidate A's tally. Another important element to keep in mind is that voting tallies are also stored as decimal fractions.

U.S. analysts questioned one of the foyers during the election of U.S. Vice President Cheney and Bush versus Kerry and Edwards, and their discovery provided clear evidence that ballots were also stored as decimal fractions. Let's break this down for those of you who aren't familiar. At the time, Kerry and Edward's tally wasn't counted as 120,360 votes but as 120,360.63. Many of the analysts gained access to the database as a direct result of court cases after candidates protested the elections.

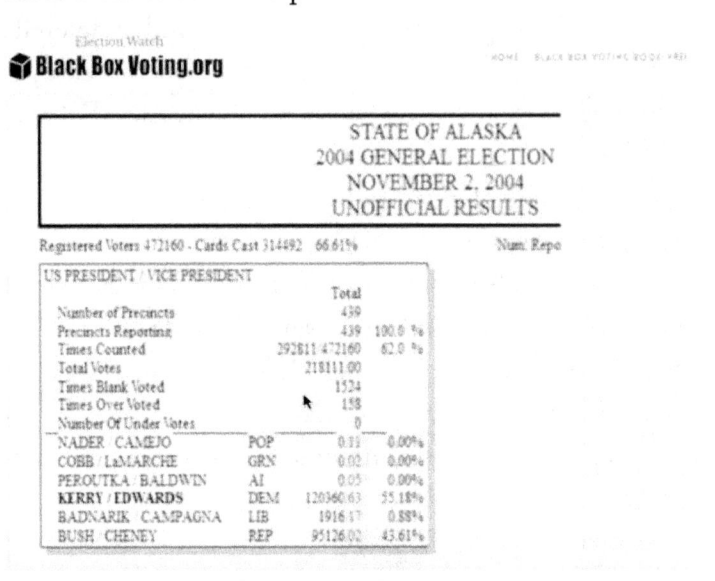

Election Watch
Black Box Voting.org

STATE OF ALASKA
2004 GENERAL ELECTION
NOVEMBER 2, 2004
UNOFFICIAL RESULTS

Registered Voters 472160 - Cards Cast 314492 66.61%

US PRESIDENT / VICE PRESIDENT		Total	
Number of Precincts		439	
Precincts Reporting		439	100.0 %
Times Counted		292811/472160	62.0 %
Total Votes		218111.00	
Times Blank Voted		1524	
Times Over Voted		158	
Number Of Under Votes		0	
NADER CAMEJO	POP	0.11	0.00%
COBB LaMARCHE	GRN	0.02	0.00%
PEROUTKA BALDWIN	AI	0.05	0.00%
KERRY / EDWARDS	**DEM**	**120360.63**	**55.18%**
BADNARIK CAMPAGNA	LIB	1916.17	0.88%
BUSH CHENEY	REP	95126.02	43.61%

Back then, candidates were less willing to sue, but there were a number of them who did, which gave them access to a specific area of information that was tabulated during the election, but unfortunately, not all of the source code. What they did discover was that votes were being stored as "double." In computer-speak, this means that the votes are stored not as whole numbers, but as a floating-point variable. Instead of 10 votes, the system will register the number as 10.54 or 10.14.

Election Watch

Black Box Voting.org   HOME BLACK BOX VOTING BOOK FREE

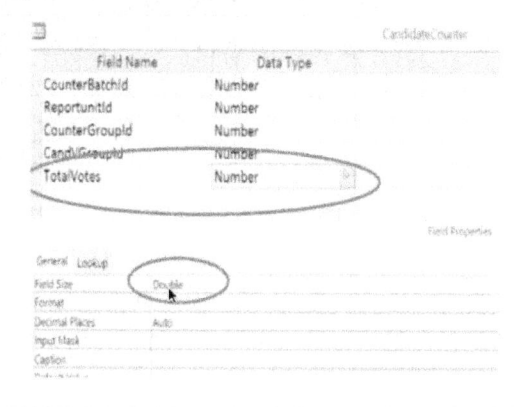

Field Name	Data Type
CounterBatchId	Number
ReportunitId	Number
CounterGroupId	Number
CandidGroupId	Number
TotalVotes	Number

Field Properties

General Lookup
Field Size   Double
Format
Decimal Places   Auto
Input Mask
Caption

The Republican candidates running in the U.S. Senate election in Massachusetts were completely bewildered at the result of the election, and knew they'd won; however, the ballot system had other ideas. The incident in Massachusetts led to a FOIA investigation whereby participating voters were tallied, meaning the number of citizens who actively voted compared with the number of ballots cast. What they found consistently across the board was that the data collected from the 7 cities showed that there was an excess of votes. To put it simply: the system registered more votes than the number of people who voted in the election.

The analysts of course found this to be very illuminating, so they dug deeper and observed the number of votes in Franklin County, which was the only county where 78% of votes were hand-counted. They found that as vote numbers proceeded, the lines representing the vote list didn't follow the trend they predicted. They expected the trend to merge and meet as the counts increased, but, in fact, in every county where the votes were machine counted, the votes didn't converge and instead displayed a parabolic effect, which is one of the big indicators that the election was compromised, and election fraud is a strong possibility.

There were many anomalies during the election, but the most noticeable of them all, and the one that started the inquiry, was Michigan. There are 86 counties in Michigan, and after analyzing the top 4 counties (Oakland County, Macomb County, Kent County, and Wayne County), analysts looked at two sets of data - the early voting data, and the voting data on Election Day.

In some instances, Kent County and Wayne County were combined, but the executive summary concluded that three of the four major counties' voter margins were reduced by a minimum of 138,000 votes for President Trump.

What that means is that Trump's total was decreased by 69,000 and Biden's vote total was increased by 69,000; simply put, the system orchestrated a 69,000-vote transfer across these Michigan counties combined. This transfer was done by a computer algorithm that linearly transferred more from Trump to Biden as the precinct increased its Republican count. The numbers varied from county to county but overall, the numbers don't lie; pooled together, the votes were more than 60,000 just in one swing state.

Another worrying discovery was that the vote transfer occurred on a higher scale in Republican-based precincts and far less in non-Republican-based precincts and Democratic strongholds, begging the question of why that would happen in such a coordinated manner.

The voting systems in Massachusetts are solely regulated as one method; however, Michigan permits two types of voting.

The first allows voters to cast their vote for an individual candidate. For example, you would walk into the precinct and say you're either voting for Biden or Trump, or Candidate A and Candidate B; regardless of the candidates, you have the freedom to vote for whomever you prefer. This is more commonly associated with independent voters who don't really align with a party and just prefer to cast their vote for an individual. The other type of voting is called Straight Party Voting, which means you enter the precinct and either vote for all Republican candidates, or you cast your vote for all Democratic candidates.

We all know that, obviously, President Trump ran as a Republican, so if a straight party vote went to the Republican party, then Donald Trump would receive that vote, whereas if the citizen went with the Democratic vote, then that ballot would go to Joe Biden. The interesting thing is, that precincts can track if voters cast either the straight party vote or the individual candidate vote.

Now, there are two types of voting at a precinct, but we'll go through an example just to clarify. Let's say 200 total voters go to a precinct and 100 of them decide to vote the straight party method. Of those straight-party votes, 60 votes are cast for the Republican candidates and 40 votes are cast for Democrat candidates – that would result in 60% Republican votes and 40% Democrat.

It's commonly agreed that based on the precinct voters who choose the straight party method, that is typically an indicator of the political party demographics within the county and that the remaining voters who selected a sole candidate aren't aligned with the party politics and maybe identify as independents.

Regarding the other 100 voters who didn't choose the straight-party voting method, let's say they chose individual candidates, and in this case, we're looking at 65 votes for Trump and 35 votes for Biden, just to keep it realistic and similar to the states we'll be analyzing. This result would give us a measurement of 65% for Donald Trump and 35% for Joe Biden.

However, now that you put it all together, you'd have the total vote count seen using both the individual ballots and the straight mark party votes. In Donald Trump's case, that would be 60 votes from the straight party pool, in addition to the 65 votes he received as a candidate, coming to a total of 125 votes or 62.5%

of the 200 votes in total. Then you take Biden's 40 votes from the Democrat straight-party tally and the 35 ballots from Biden's total, giving us 75, which translates to 37.5%.

That's how the news would report the count and that's how most precincts conduct their tallying systems. This is merely an example to give you an understanding of the straight-party voting method, the individual method, and how they combine to give the election officials a figure. The analysis that was performed compared two very specific metrics. The metrics were plotted on the X-axis and the Y-axis of a graph. On the X-axis, you'll find the Republican straight-party votes for each precinct, and on the Y-axis, you'll find direct Trump candidate votes, which means how many people voted directly for Trump, and not the rest of the Republican party.

To explain how they analyzed the data, we're going to use the first precinct alphabetically as the example, which is Ada Township Precinct 1, and in the 2020 U.S. election, 1075 people voted in that precinct. That includes people who voted early and voted on Election Day. We've already covered that when you vote in Michigan, you've got a choice - you can walk in and just say I want to vote for this party, be it Republican, Democrat, or any of the other parties.

What you're saying is for President, for Senate, for the House of Representatives, and everyone on the ticket, you just want to vote for whatever candidates belong to that party. At Ada Township, 564 people did that, and from that number, 307 voted for Republicans.

The first step is to calculate all the people who voted by party and what percent voted Republican. Now separately, the other 511 people took the more arduous option of individually picking every single candidate that they wanted to vote for down the ticket, and they could mix and match between the parties if they want to. In the case of Ada Township, 165 picked Trump in the presidential segment of the election, which is 32.3%.

Ada Township Precinct 1
1,075

564
307 GOP
= 54.4%

511
165 TRUMP
= 32.3%

vote by party | vote by candidate

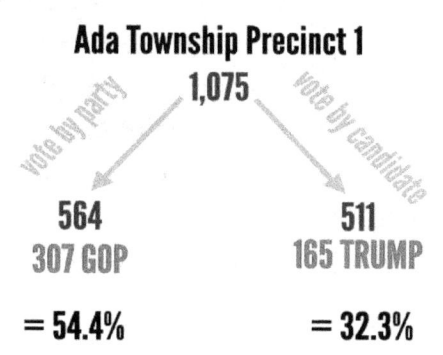

What we now do is calculate the difference between those two figures. You can see based on the graph there's a negative 22.1% difference when we plot the percentage of people who voted for Republican by party line against the percentage of people who "voted by the candidate" for Trump.

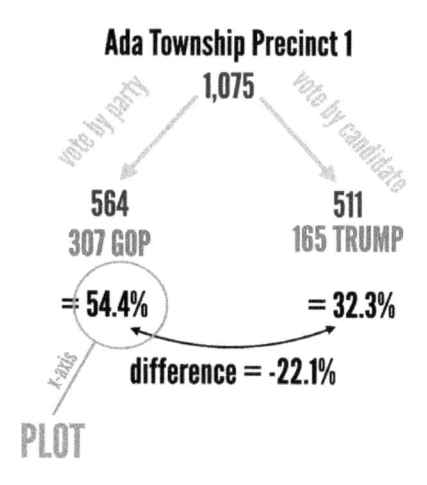

Ada Township Precinct 1
1,075

564
307 GOP
= 54.4%

511
165 TRUMP
= 32.3%

vote by party | vote by candidate

difference = -22.1%

x-axis

PLOT

Apply that for all 252 precincts in Kent County, and we get this scatter plot. When you apply this line of fit, which goes across, first of all, and then down, the details of why exactly the line goes across first are more about what is expected compared to the trend we note on the graph. Even by switching to a standard line of best fit to suit the more liberal agenda, the main theory is the slope going down and not horizontal.

The analyst's theory is that if you take a precinct and you look at the position of people who vote by party and then vote Republican, that gives you a sense of how people vote in that area, which means it should be a good predictor.

Correlate with the percentage of people who vote for a candidate, who then also picked Trump, and the idea is if they are closely linked, this should be a very small difference in the percentage between them. So, in principle, this line should be flat – but it's not. The fact that it's not flat and that it slopes down is taken as an indication that votes have been stolen, that the line should be higher, and the votes now gone down the line give the signal that something went askew.

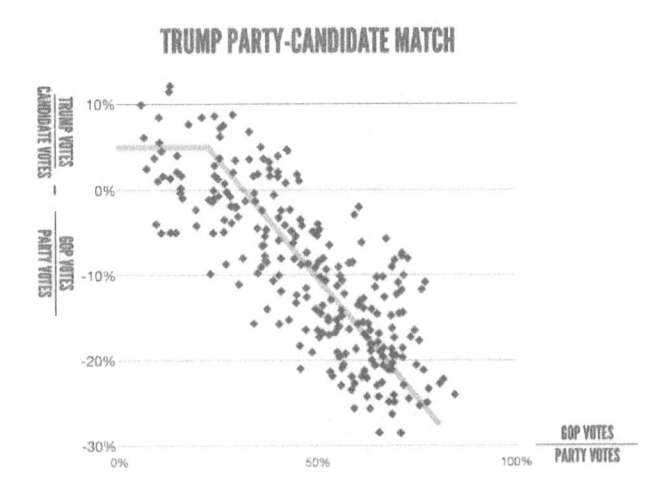

TRUMP PARTY-CANDIDATE MATCH

This was one of the biggest anomalies at the time and sent many federal candidates into a state of confusion as they watched the graph fight every indicator that the county was theirs for the taking.

CHAPTER 6

Blaming the voting machines which count the votes, with Dominion Voting Systems taking a lot of the heat, was a vital component in uncovering the many frauds that had taken place, but before we get into the brunt of the meddling, it's important to point out the allegations that were discredited or false, for historical accuracy.

In this chapter, I'll take you through a quick rundown of what happened to the security of the election during the run-up to election night and how the people regulating the ballot tallies did more harm than the machines themselves. We've already covered the principles of U.S. election law and how people can cast their vote; however, it is worth explaining the current system of voting in the U.S. and how electronic voting machines play a role in the system.

Because elections are run by states and not the federal government, obviously there's quite a bit of variation depending on numerous factors, but in general, you can break electronic voting down into two categories

1. The most common is voting using an optical scan system, wherein you fill out marks on a piece of paper and the paper is subsequently scanned by a machine, very similar to the scantrons often used in schools and standard tests.
2. This isn't as common as voting with a direct recording machine. Here your ballot is entirely digitally filled out on a machine leaving no paper trail, meaning if something goes wrong, you'll have very little physical evidence of those errors.

Now we know how the system currently works, it's also worth discussing some of the known issues with the system because as we've already disclosed, these machines aren't reliable, especially in the wrong hands.

The main issue often cited by election officials, somewhat ironically, is trust. Digital voting just feels less trustworthy and becomes even more problematic when you're using a direct recording system because now you don't have a paper trail to fall back on. You're just crossing your fingers and hoping that the programmers didn't screw something up. You should know by now that most issues aren't scary hackers, but sleep-deprived and biased election workers who "accidentally" press the wrong button during the count. Innocent mistakes do occur, but these faults are commonly just a front for more sinister actions. As innocent as such mistakes may seem to the average citizen, they still create an issue when there's no paper trail and can lead to major disparities in totals.

These problems have been raised before, but they've never gained significant traction because they've never had an integral advocate like President Trump before. Though Trump was not complaining about the issue back in the 2016 election, this time, the president knew there was something wrong, making the case that he lost the election because of fraudulent voting machines and illegal votes being counted, which was correct.

So, what was it that led to the Trump campaign looking elsewhere for wrongdoing, instead of the obvious? Well, as we've already covered, the voting machines leave very little evidence to support allegations of misconduct and fraud, meaning the Trump campaign had a hard time bringing these allegations to lawful fruition.

The core claim made by Trump and others is that Dominion's voting machines were rigged against the president, with them allegedly deleting millions of Trump votes and changing thousands of others from Trump to Biden.

ONON said at the time that "they got this information from an unaudited analysis of data conducted by Edison Research."

The problem with this avenue was that their president said Edison Research had produced no such report and had no evidence of any voter fraud. So, with Edison denying the claim, they were asked to provide further evidence, which was an impossibility.

Then there were the issues in Antrim County. In the Michigan county, the results were initially tabulated incorrectly, giving Biden a 3000-vote win in the ordinarily red area. Officials spotted the issue, looked into it, and found that, in reality, Trump had won Antrim by 2500 votes, but Biden was given a win in a county that used Dominion voting machines, clear evidence of machines flipping votes for Biden. Well, not exactly.

The actual problem was humans flipping votes for Biden. As the Michigan secretary of state pointed out, the error had nothing to do with the machines and instead was a "human error," saying the equipment and software did not malfunction and all ballots were properly tabulated; however, the clerk "accidentally" failed to update the software used to collect voting machine data and reported unofficial results. Similar claims were made in Georgia too, with people like Sean Hannity saying that there have been issues in the state. And as the Georgia secretary of state made clear, despite there being some reporting delays, the machines had counted every ballot correctly. So, what was it? Well, you guessed it – human interference. Although Trump was right in his intuition, the actual cause of the injustice was far less innocent.

A voting technology expert from the nonpartisan OSET institute who monitored more than 1000 reports of voter issues since Election Day felt that there were only a small handful of issues and that most issues were the result of "human error" involving voting systems, not the software itself.

Trump also mentioned a serious issue in an infamous tweet, proposing that 941,000 Trump votes in Pennsylvania had been deleted by Dominion. Now, this was perhaps where the President sacrificed his bishop instead of a pawn. A mistake on that scale isn't easy to cover up, and we can only surmise that one of Trump's advisors wasn't there to counsel patience before the claim was made.

The problem is that it's mathematically impossible. The technology systems were used in 14 Pennsylvania counties, counting a total of 1.3 million Pennsylvanian votes, a 76% turnout. Using that information, we can work out the maximum number of ballots that could have been cast was 1.7 million. So, throwing away 940,000 would surely be noticed. Considering that 52% of the votes that Dominion counted for Trump were some 676,000, it would have been mathematically impossible for them to throw away 941,000 Trump votes, alter 221,000, but still count 676,000 in addition. That's simply more votes than the size of the total electorate. However, as mentioned in the previous chapter, machines were guilty of transferring votes, not exactly moving them from the board.

Trump's hastiness may have cost him much of his credibility in many of these claims, but the Democrats were yet to notice one of their biggest blunders, which would go on to become the very core of the many lawsuits the Republicans would file following the election. This undisputed transgression from the Democratic Party warranted unlawful changes to election policy running up to the voting period and not stopping until the very night of counting. This is an issue that has been recognized by both sides as unlawful, and in turn, cost the Democrats severely in the public realm.

Many of you are probably already aware of what I'm referring to, but for those of you unaware at the time, let me give you a rundown of each lawsuit and the details of each dispute following the 2020 election.

During the following weeks after election night, Republicans noticed many election irregularities in the six states where Joe Biden led the vote count, alleging in the lawsuits and public statements that election officials did not follow proper procedures while counting ballots. As absentee ballots helped Biden overtake Trump in Pennsylvania, Republicans sought to stop Philadelphia officials from counting them, claiming that GOP observers had been barred from the rooms where the votes were being counted. That is not legal in the State of Pennsylvania.

The Trump campaign repeated this claim in another federal lawsuit, adding that standards for verifying mail ballots were applied unevenly across the state in a way that disadvantaged Republicans. The suit sought to block certification of election results in the state on an emergency basis. Trump's team saw a few small victories in the state, though none came close to affecting the race's outcome.

The campaign won an order to move observers closer to the counting machines in Philadelphia, which succeeded in getting Supreme Court Justice Samuel A. Alito Jr. to issue an order that election officials must separate ballots that arrived after Election Day but before the Friday evening — a step that counties had to abide by. Under an earlier ruling by the State Supreme Court, election officials could tally those ballots, which were a tiny fraction of the overall vote, but state officials ordered them to be kept segregated in case of further legal challenges.

A judge who questioned Pennsylvania mail-in vote law enacted in 2020 who tried to halt additional steps needed to certify the state's 2020 election results said the Pennsylvania legislature's "expansion of mail-in voting enacted over a year earlier was likely illegal." Commonwealth court judge Patricia McCullough's November 25 order was blocked by the Pennsylvania Supreme Court while it considered the case filed by state Republicans. The case was unrelated to the one brought by President Donald Trump's campaign which was rejected by a federal appeals court that sought to undo Pennsylvania's certification of president-elect Joe Biden's victory in the keystone state after evidence of misconduct. Patricia McCullough's statement also missed the point.

What Patricia McCullough was arguing was that the legislative expansion of the mail-in voting (done by a Republican legislature) was likely unconstitutional as it requires a constitutional amendment, not simply the passing of legislation. What was really at issue in Pennsylvania was Democrat Governor Wolf's changing of election integrity and security protocols related to signatures, postmarks, backdating of receipts, adjudication, etc. The relaxing of those protocols is not legally done by the executive branch. It must have come from the legislative branch, which it did not. Therefore, every vote counted in violation of the legislative authority, but following the perceived executive branch authority, was **illegal**. This accounts for hundreds of thousands of votes in Pennsylvania.

Elsewhere in Pennsylvania, Republicans sued to stop local election officials from releasing the names of voters whose absentee ballots had been rejected for errors such as a lack of signature and authentication. The Supreme Court also ruled to allow Pennsylvania to accept mail-in ballots received up to three days after Election Day. The Court's decision followed a Pennsylvania Supreme Court ruling requiring boards of elections to count mail-in ballots postmarked by November 3rd and received by November 6th. Following the state court ruling, the Republican Party of Pennsylvania appealed to the Supreme Court to overturn the ruling; however, the Court declined to take up the Republican Party's challenge, leaving the original ruling in place. Such a change would drastically shape the outcome of Pennsylvania. Coupling together the power to backdate non-postmarked ballots with the court's ruling (Democrat-controlled) created a position where the Court and the Governor colluded together to count hundreds of thousands of votes that constitutionally and legislatively were **illegal**.

Trump's lawyer, Rudolph W. Giuliani, stated that the campaign was prepared to file another lawsuit, alleging wrongdoing on a grand scale in Pennsylvania. "Many cases are going to be filed, some big, some small. This is going to eventually be a big case." This ultimately would become a part of the larger U.S. Supreme Court, which was dismissed for lack of "standing." In reality, standing existed because if one state follows its own rules and other states do not, it creates an interstate disenfranchising of its voting population - a clear constitutional crisis for the rights of citizens between states and clear constitutional harm to those citizens. Standing was meant.

So how did the U.S. Supreme Court get this dismissal so wrong? Courts traditionally try to avoid being involved in election issues to avoid the appearance of bias. If the U.S. Supreme Court had reviewed the merits of the case, it is extremely likely they would agree with the position that illegal votes should not be counted. This would have flipped the swing states from Biden to Trump - and likely caused severe social unrest. The U.S. Supreme Court chose the path of least resistance, and in effect, "sold out" the principles of the Constitution to preserve social stability. Some argue this was a wise decision in the face of unprecedented circumstances; others called this cowardly.

In Michigan, Biden trailed on election night, but then, as in other Midwestern states, surged back to overtake Trump as thousands of ballots were counted, seemingly out of nowhere.

In three lawsuits, Republicans alleged that there was impropriety in those ballot counts. They lost, both times, after judges claimed Republicans could not provide evidence of wrongdoing, despite tangible evidence from the numerous voting stations.

Justice Samuel Alito, joined by Justices Clarence Thomas and Neil Gorsuch, suggested that the court may still revisit the case after the election and toss out contested mail-in ballots. Although the Supreme Court declined to rule on the matter before the election, Alito wrote that there was a "strong likelihood that the State Supreme Court decision violates the Federal Constitution." As usual, the Court continued without care.

In another case, Republicans said GOP election observers in Detroit were being excluded when city officials fixed, or "cured," ballots that their machines couldn't read. In these cases — which might be caused by a stray mark or a coffee stain — officials can make a duplicate ballot, with the same votes, and run that one instead. Republicans said they had "information and belief" that this curing process had been done repeatedly without a GOP official there to observe it. They asked a judge to delay certifying Detroit's results.

Trump's presidential campaign also asked a judge to stop all processing of absentee ballots in Michigan. In that case, a Republican election observer said she'd been given a sticky note by an unnamed poll worker, alleging that late-arriving ballots were being counted improperly.

Meanwhile, RNC Chairwoman Ronna McDaniel raised another series of claims during a news conference in Bloomfield Hills, alleging that election workers in Detroit were told to backdate certain ballots. Detroit officials denied the accusation, putting an abrupt end to the investigation.

McDaniel acknowledged that her allegations had not been fully vetted and said the information had been shared with federal prosecutors. A Justice Department official said the information McDaniel provided had been referred to the FBI. It was unclear what action, if any, the agency planned to take. An FBI spokeswoman in Detroit referred a reporter to the U.S. attorney's office, which declined to comment.

The allegation about backdating was part of a suit filed in which two GOP poll challengers asked a judge to block the city of Detroit from certifying its election results. Their complaint cited an account from another woman, who said she was a city ballot counting employee claiming she was told to enter incorrect data into a voter-tracking system.

That allegation was focused on absentee ballots, which the state required to arrive by 8:00 PM on Election Day. The city employee, Jessy Jacob, said that after Election Day, supervisors told her to enter data into a computer system to show that some absentee ballots had arrived before the deadline. Jacob said she felt that was improper, implying that the ballots might have been backdated after missing the deadline. In her follow-up news conference, McDaniel also asserted that 2,000 Republican ballots in Rochester Hills had been "given to Democrats due to a clerical error."

In Georgia, Trump's campaign filed a lawsuit the day after the election, focusing narrowly on absentee ballots in Chatham County, home to Savannah. The campaign asked that any absentee ballots arriving after polls closed on Tuesday be set aside. For most voters, Georgia required ballots to arrive before the end of Election Day, though there's an exception for military voters and overseas voters. The Trump campaign cited an affidavit from a poll worker who said he thought he might have seen late-arriving ballots improperly mingled with ones cast on time. Even if that was true, it was not an election-changing problem. The allegation dealt with a small number of ballots in a single county.

In Arizona, the Trump campaign and the Republican National Committee filed suit in state court alleging that poll workers pushed or told some voters to push a button on a tabulating machine to cast their ballot, even after machine tabulators had detected an "overvote" — that is, the machine detected the possibility that the person had voted for two candidates.

Under state rules, they said, voters are supposed to be allowed to cancel such ballots and try again because, sometimes, stray ink marks or smudges can cause the tabulator to improperly assess an "overvote." The campaign asked a judge to order a manual review of such ballots and to bar the certification of the Arizona vote until it is complete.

In Nevada, two days after the election, a group of Trump allies claimed that thousands of people had voted illegally in Clark County, home to Las Vegas. Neither the Trump campaign nor the GOP was named plaintiff in the federal lawsuit that was eventually filed by Republicans, which failed to present evidence that thousands of people had voted improperly. By then, the allegation had been whittled down drastically. Instead of 10,000 cases, Trump's allies presented one: a woman named Jill Stokke, who said she was denied the right to vote in person because her mail ballot had been stolen and filled out by someone else.

The Trump allies wanted U.S. District Judge Andrew Gordon to order a ban on the use of a machine for verifying signatures, a move that would have slowed down an already slow count. He did not. Instead, Gordon told the plaintiffs to return to court if they found more evidence to back their claims. Beyond that lawsuit, GOP officials also alleged that more than 3,000 people voted in Nevada despite not living in the state.

Lawyers for the Trump campaign sent a letter to U.S. Attorney General William P. Barr alleging "criminal voter fraud in the State of Nevada" and claiming to have identified 3,062 people who voted improperly. They enclosed a list of addresses of voters who they said had moved out of state; the information, they said, came from cross-checking voter data with the National Change of Address database. At a later news conference, Trump campaign officials went further, claiming that as many as 9,000 non-residents wrongly voted and that the Clark County elections system was riddled with other fraud.

In Wisconsin, the Trump campaign said that it was continuing with plans to seek a recount of the results in Wisconsin, where unofficial tallies show Biden leading Trump by about 20,500 votes, a 0.6% margin of victory. The state allows a candidate to request a recount if the margin of a race is under 1%, but the campaign must pay unless it is under 0.25%. Under Wisconsin law, a recount petition in a presidential election cannot be filed until all counties complete a canvass of local results.

The Michigan and Pennsylvania rulings also involved multiple other voting-related policies. The Pennsylvania court ruled in favor of drop boxes for returning mail-in ballots and removed Green Party candidates from the ballot, while the Michigan court struck down a ban on outside groups driving voters to the polls. Michigan ballots were also eligible to be counted if they were postmarked by the day before Election Day and received within 14 days after November 3rd. A judge extended the state's deadline for receiving mail-in ballots, a move likely to reduce the number of ballots rejected for lateness, but which could delay results in some races in the battleground state court of claims, which as we now know did indeed occur.

Voters in several swing states had more leeway in getting their mail ballots back in time to count during the election due to prior rule changes. The changes, however, would go on to delay the reporting of election results and set up court fights down the line. In North Carolina, a settlement announced by the State Board of Elections said ballots postmarked by Election Day would count if officials received them within nine days after the election. And in Wisconsin, a federal judge similarly ruled that ballots postmarked by Election Day would count if officials had them in hand within six days after November 3rd. Pennsylvania's Supreme Court said ballots that are postmarked on or before Election Day will be counted so long as they're received within the next three days. And a Michigan state judge also ruled that absentee ballots postmarked by November 3rd can be counted if they arrive up to two weeks after Election Day.

The developments meant that more votes counted in the states that would have otherwise been disqualified, giving Biden an edge in the election due to the sheer number of Biden supporters who planned to vote by mail. It also meant a longer wait before a definitive winner was announced in the closely contested battlegrounds, which left millions of voters waiting weeks before any results were disclosed.

These instances raged on from December to well into 2021. Scarcely broadcast on the mainstream channels, due to the undisputed nature of the lawsuits, the details were left untouched, and in turn, the Trump campaign was mocked for their tenacity in revealing the truth. Unfortunately for them, the courts had other ideas and would have rather kept their careers and pensions instead of helping to uncover the hundreds of policy changes, human interferences, and unlawful behaviors that stretched from September 2020 to November 2020.

CHAPTER 7

Not long after the election, the public of Georgia was presented with footage. Footage that reported ballot counting, clearly exposing volunteers meddling with the tabulation of the ballots. The information presented at the time came from two Republican field organizers who were sent to Fulton County to be observers. However, at no time were they permitted to observe appropriately, instead being subjugated and forced to stand off to the side, roped off with Fox News.

In the video, two observers arrive in the morning, appearing on camera around 8:00 AM to begin watching the tabulation of absentee and military ballots. But according to their affidavits, around the time of 10:00 PM, one person working the polls told everyone in the room to leave on the basis that they were going to stop counting and return at 8:30 AM to continue counting. Who was this person? And why did she tell people to leave? It was for a "water main" leak - that never existed.

What was evident from the footage was that at 10:00 PM, there were numerous workers present counting the ballots, and in the very back corner, the Republican observers and the press were visible. So, according to the witnesses (the Republican observers), a lady with blonde braids working as part of the count team announced they were going to stop counting and that everyone should go home. This has since been confirmed as indisputable, and since the footage was released, others have come forward attesting to this claim.

Following this call to halt the count, everyone cleared out, including the Republican observers in the press box. However, four people stayed behind and continued counting and tabulating well into the night. This procedure was carried out unobserved and unsupervised – not in public view as the statute requires. This illegal act continued until about 1:00 AM without anybody else entering the room. To be clear, the Georgia law stipulates those partisan observers may or may not observe, but they are entitled to observe if they wish. They were forcibly removed, meaning every vote counted unsupervised was **illegal**.

The only reason this managed to get out into the public was that when the Republican observers were forced to leave, they went to the central tabulation center, and they got word from a news crew that ballot counting had continued indefinitely without observation. Obviously, to them, this came as a surprise. The fact that not everybody left the room according to what was planned by the workers meant that either those people still counting were deaf, or they were committing illegal activity. This information shocked them, so they returned to State Farm Arena at about 1:00 AM where they confirmed that people had just left State Farm arena in contravention of what had been told by the supervisors who were running the ballot operation.

After reviewing the video, officials could see the change at 10:25 PM. They watched the room fill up and turn into a bustling environment earlier in the day, and then just before 10:30 PM, everybody clears out, which is consistent with what the affidavits said. The intent was made clear when people were told to go home and come back at 8:30 AM. They said we will now stop working and stop counting. Who stays behind? You have these four mysterious people, like I said, consistent with the affidavits that were documented shortly after the day of tabulation.

The people involved all seemed to have their jobs within the operation. The woman in purple and the two women in yellow were centered towards the back of the room, which was where the scanners were located. The woman with the blonde braids who told everyone to leave appeared at the time to be something of a ringleader, and we'll get to why in just a moment. So, the four women remained, just as the Republican observers said. The observers were indeed the last people to leave the State Farm arena along with the Fox News crew, except the four accomplices who managed to stay behind after the 10:30 PM emptying.

Soon after the majority of people left the room, the women in yellow began just sitting still for a while; ostensibly not working because, after all, they said they were going to stop counting, and stop counting they did. But they didn't wait long. Only long enough for the witnesses to leave the room along with the rest of the press. That was when we saw them move into action and once again begin scanning ballots. The women in yellow seemed to stand out more, but what caught everybody's eye were the other two women, the one in purple and the one wearing the blue apron with the blonde braids.

What happened soon after, at around 11:00 PM, was the primary source that confirmed the tabulation was dishonest. One of the ladies reaches underneath a table and reveals an entire box of ballots, hidden under the cloth. Now, at first, people weren't aware as to how the ballots were stored and if this was the correct conduct. Observing footage from earlier in the day shows the boxes of ballots coming through the door and then steadily being circulated throughout the room as time passes – not to be hidden beneath tables. At the time, it was a little confusing because they were stored in these black containers, and the room is also home to many U.S. Postal Service containers, so it was all a little messy. All Republicans wanted to know at the time was whether or not they were indeed legitimate ballots being retrieved from the cover of a table. Where did the ballots come from? Who put the ballots there, underneath a table? When did they conceal them? And most importantly of all, why?

The ballots that were pulled out from underneath the table were placed there in the early hours of the day at around 8:20 AM. The woman who placed the ballots under the table is the same woman who told everyone to clear out of the room later that very day. Therefore, it was initially suspected that she was something of a ringleader during this attempted fraud. It was the exact same person who stayed behind after clearing the place out under the pretense that people were going to stop counting that had also placed the table and ballots beneath it at 8:22 in the morning. Overall, the video showed four suitcases (later argued "black boxes"; however, one of the "boxes" is a wheeled suitcase, which is where the idea originated from) that were taken from beneath the table.

The question at the time was, what were these ballots doing separate from all the other ballots? And why are they only counting them whenever the place is cleared out with no witnesses? We've already established that the ballot machines can process thousands of ballots in a short amount of time - about 3,000 ballots per hour to be precise. In this particular room, there were multiple machines available for use, and the workers who stayed behind were counting from 11:00 PM all the way to just after 1:00 AM. The math is irrefutable and caused a massive uproar at the time.

Just how many ballots went through those machines in those two hours when there was nobody around to supervise consistently with statutes and rules when supervising tabulation? It was believed at the time that this period was more than enough time to extend a margin of victory and turn the tide. The video also clearly shows the ballots of the four boxes being run through the system multiple times (3-4 times each stack of ballots). This is unusual behavior and can lead to multi-counting of the ballots. In addition to the four workers that were seen on video, two other people were bringing ballots in and out of the room. A gentleman in red and then a second person who couldn't be identified at the time. But in total, there were 6 accomplices, and it appeared on initial viewing that the woman with the blonde braids and blue apron was fronting the operation.

They were scanning until about 12:55 in the morning, when the Republican observers who provided the affidavits reappeared after hearing about this illegal activity through news coverage. At that time, just as they said in their affidavit, it was around 1:00 AM when the witnesses discovered that the counting had continued unsupervised, and so they returned between 1:30 AM and 1:45 AM. Not only was this done covertly, but the witnesses also claimed that they had to fight through security to get into the center but eventually they managed to enter. In their affidavits, it was two different people who affirmed for them that people had been counting from just after 10:30 in the evening when they cleared out, right up until approximately 5 minutes before they arrived, and that they had the names of those people on record.
Now, at the time there was confusion as to what exactly the lady with the blonde braids said, which was a complete contradiction to what they were told by employees from Fulton County. The lady with the blonde braids was quickly becoming the center of this investigation. Because the discovery was so soon after the election, the identity of the woman was still a mystery. The witnesses simply gave the descriptions, and because of her distinctive appearance, people could easily make out clearly who she was based on the other people in the room.

Remember, it was the lady in the blonde braids halfway down her back who yelled out that everyone must leave and stop counting. The Fulton County spokesperson didn't have names for the Republicans investigating the incident. All that was discernible was the name "Ruby" across the shirt of the lady in purple. It was only because of these affidavits that people knew which leads to follow and who to talk to. You might even recall that the press reported a supposed pipe break in the vicinity, which they quickly used as an excuse for people clearing out of the State Farm arena, though that was never mentioned in the affidavits from the people who were present in the room. This later turned out to be a minor leak in a bathroom stall that was easily turned off and placed out of order.

Officials didn't know at the time what was at play. All they noticed was that the table wasn't there earlier in the day, but it soon arrived in the hands of the braided lady, who would then go on to obscure the location of the ballots under the table.

Following the discovery, all Republican officials had to go off was the woman who moved the table and the ballots and told everyone to leave. The problem was she was dressed differently in the morning, so it took many hours to determine if it was the same person or just a look-alike. To their luck, it was the same person in the evening dressed in the blue apron, who later yelled for everyone to leave. The same woman who stays behind to help tabulate ballots after they've all left, she's the one who chose to place the table so close to the scanners, and she was the lead they needed.

In Georgia, Trump's campaign sued in an attempt to block some absentee ballots from arriving after the polls had closed. The campaign claimed it had major concerns about a couple of thousand votes in Chatham County. For most Georgia voters, the deadline to submit their ballots was before the end of Election Day. The exception is for military and overseas voters. The Trump campaign later claimed that a poll worker saw multiple late-arriving ballots in one county.

After the footage of the lady pulling out hidden boxes stuffed with ballots was made public, the footage was analyzed, and the two women turned out to be related. The mother, dressed in the purple shirt, was named Ruby Freeman, and her daughter, the infamous lady in blonde braids, was identified as election supervisor, Moss. The video was then handed over and reviewed, revealing that Freeman had scanned the same stack of ballots repeatedly. Surveillance cameras showed clearly that these two poll workers watched and waited until the Republican observers and reporters had left the room at 10:30 PM before they resumed scanning ballots. These two workers along with the other two workers in yellow then continued counting uninterrupted for almost three hours until after 1:00 AM.

During this time, Ruby Freeman repeatedly scanned the same batch of ballots at least three times, which is illegal, and this was all captured on tape. Freeman was working closely with her daughter, Moss, who was also caught on camera as the apparent ringleader behind the fraud. Georgia's officials made serious efforts to dismiss the evidence presented on the videos, yet there was no explanation as to why Freeman scanned the same ballots multiple times, nor why they remained behind while the rest of the building was evacuated. Lawyers said it was "highly unusual" for anyone to store suitcases/boxes full of ballots under tablecloths, and it was "not unclear when those cases were delivered" or "why Ruby Freeman and her daughter waited until Republican observers left before they opened them.." Based on the number of ballots observed in the cases and the number of times Ruby scanned the same set of ballots, experts claimed they could easily have accounted for the sudden spike in votes for candidate Joe Biden. Oddly enough, the strange spikes that are statistically virtually impossible are correlated at the same time - 10:30 PM to 1:00 AM.

The Biden administration did all it could to fight against these claims, not just the new voter integrity laws, but also audits in Georgia, essentially trying to do a grand cover-up of their failings. However, despite this, a patriotic group in Georgia, as a result of pressing for information, was able to obtain the provable evidence of illegality, and almost instantly, Trump was all over the details. He issued a statement mere hours after the information leaked that the news coming out of Georgia was beyond incredible and proof of voter illegality. The former President said: "The hand recount in Fulton County was a total fraud. They stuffed the ballot box and got caught. We will lose our country if this is allowed to stand."

Trump's spokesman, Liz Harrington, was busier than anybody the following day, putting out information, almost by the hour, in the form of bombshell images that greatly aided the Trump effort. "Whistle-blower takes photos of stacks of supposed mail-in ballots, but they don't have any creases," she stated after the news dropped. "Never in an envelope and they look like they were all photocopied." She also said there were some ballot batch-sheets (with photos) saying: "Unanimous 100 to 0, 150 to 0, 200 to 0, all for Biden. Extremely fishy." She then went on to say there were countless votes in Fulton County, counted more than once, the very ballots counted by Moss and Freeman, issuing the same vote on two separate occasions, as we covered in previous chapters.

Now, of course, we saw some of this right in the aftermath of November 2020, and all of it seemed to sort of vanish and go nowhere beyond the void of Twitter. Why, you ask? Well, simply because it was, by itself, dismissed as "anecdotal" (think of that when there is video surveillance of counting happening after removing monitors, which is on its face illegal). There were cases here and there, but they always failed to amount to anything more than speculation on social media. What it did add up to, however, was Biden's margin of victory shrinking by 2,525 votes.

Now, Trump lost Georgia by 12,000 votes, so this would not be enough by itself to overturn a decision like Georgia. Yet just because the election wasn't decided by Georgia, it doesn't negate the fact that 6+ other swing states also faced the same challenges as Georgia. The point is, the Republicans were correct to say the audit was only examined on a marginal scale, that only a tiny portion of the ballots was looked at. It was only the hand recount, and right away what Republicans saw were severe documented problems, and in some cases, provable fraud to the most accurate degree. The group called VoterGA were the people who pressed to get all this information and also pressed the Georgia assembly to make the information public.

What I did note while writing this was that, interestingly, the Atlanta Journal-Constitution, a very left-wing institution (in practice, the New York Times of Atlanta), wrote an article on the front page. The article was entitled "Some ballots initially double-counted." This was very surprising to me considering how much of this information was covered up by Big Tech and other major news outlets. If you try to find any of this on Google or Firefox, you'll find yourself scrolling through pages upon pages of left-wing material, all of which adamantly discourages any form of rebuttal. So, you even have an acknowledgment from the left, which on a good day is hard to achieve. Then, in the same article, the discovery of identical ballots provides evidence to back up allegations of serious fraud. And I should say that "problems," when stated here, is a code word for fraud and illegality.

But of course, they will always try to cover their tracks. And so, it goes on, "but on a relatively small scale that had no bearing on the final certified count." In essence, the true intent of the piece was to agree halfway to avoid losing too much credibility, which looking back, was the smart move. However, this by itself doesn't settle the case; the question now is, were there more to be uncovered, and if so, was there enough to seriously alter the course of the election? To predict before we get into the evidence in full, let's get into the weeds of the tangle. Fulton County was talking about the mail-in absentee ballots and essentially looking at the mail-in absentee ballots. Where did they come from? How many were counted? How many were fraudulent? VoterGA said they were "riddled with massive errors and provable fraud." They looked at Fulton County's hand count audit, which was, by the way, held November 14th and 15th 2020, and they found "a whopping 60% error rate."

Just think about that for a second. When you have a 60% error rate, more than half the ballots hand-counted were being miscounted. I'm now just going to spell out the details because I want to make sure this is completely accurate. Of the batch, there were 15,139 batch files, which contained 100 mail-in ballots each; 60% of them contained errors.

Several batch files of mail-in ballots were redundantly added into the audit results, including extra vote totals of 3,390 votes for Biden, 865 for trump, and 43 for a third candidate. VoterGA says that it was not simply a case of errors. Why? Well, because VoterGA found "7 falsified audit tally sheets containing fabricated vote totals." So, to give you an idea, the seven batches of valid images had votes that totaled 705 votes; 554 went for Biden, and 140 went for Trump. That was the actual number. So, in an urban area, it's not surprising that Biden was ahead. He got 554, and Trump received 140. But when they finalized the audit totals, the result tallied 850 for Biden, and 0 for Donald Trump. Fulton altered the totals, giving all the votes, including Trump's votes, to President Biden. Let's continue. Fulton County also failed to include tally sheets for 100,000 ballots, of which more than 50,000 were mail-in ballots, and they claimed that they didn't have them, or at least they didn't have them on hand and so were incapable of producing them. There were also 200 Fulton County mail-in-ballot images containing votes that weren't even counted or registered.

So, on the one hand, you have votes that are counted wrong, and on the other hand, you have votes that were cast but not even registered or included in the official count. All of this was a sharp contradiction to the Georgia Secretary of State Brad Raffensperger, a Republican, who claimed that the process was extremely secure, there was no mismatch, and the recount that occurred essentially corresponded precisely with the original count, making this a clean election in Georgia. This completely negates the facts. So, what we saw in Fulton County was manifestly not the case in any way, but a complete betrayal of the truth. All of this indicated to me and those around me that we needed to probe further and dive deeper, and to turn stones over (or tables for that matter) and look under them for other hidden frauds.

These were not the only instances of illegality and irregularity in the 2020 presidential election in Georgia. VoterGA created the following executive summary of the myriad issues in Georgia that demand accountability:

- The U.S. District Court found on October 11th, 2020 that the Dominion Voting System that was used in the November 2020 election was unverifiable to the voter and in violation of two Georgia statutes;
- There are six sworn affidavits of counterfeit mail-in ballots in Fulton Co. election results scaling into the tens of thousands;
- The State Farm Arena video shows at least four violations of Georgia election law;
- Approximately 43,000 DeKalb Co. drop box ballots have no chain of custody forms to authenticate them with;
- Tru-Vote Geo tracking showed evidence of ballot harvesting teams driving repeatedly to drop boxes in Fulton and DeKalb;
- All 350,000+ original in-person ballot images in Fulton are missing in violation of federal and state retention law;
- All 393,000+ original ballot images in Cobb are missing in violation of federal and state retention law;
- At least 17,720 certified in-person recount votes have no ballot images in Fulton;
- 18,325 voters had vacant residential addresses according to the U.S. Post Office;

- 904 voters were registered at a P.O. Box address, which is illegal;
- All or large parts of 2,000,000 original ballot images from 70+ Georgia counties are missing;
- Failure to make mandatory check of ballot envelope signature to the signature on file resulted in a 2020 absentee ballot rejection rate drop from 3.47% (in 2018) to 0.34%, which translates to the acceptance and inclusion of approximately 4,400 dubious Fulton County mail-in ballots;
- The U.S. District Court found Georgia's secretary of state's office "not credible" on August 16th, 2019;
- A report compiled by Matt Braynard and his team at Look Ahead America provided specific, verifiable evidence that likely illegal ballots exceed the margin of victory in the presidential race;
- Statistical abnormalities identified in many GA counties by former Army Intelligence Captain Seth Keschel show that it is implausible that the election results are correct.

Now realize that the left, the media, has been trying to create this false sense of unanimity after the election, claiming that everything has already been decided and that the counts are not only final but completely irrefutable. What they're doing and have been doing for the past 12 months is trying to lull us into a sense of complacency, and luckily, I find that Republican voters haven't been fooled by these attempts to discourage and warp the truth. We saw it clear as day. We saw the anomalies around the election, and we're not convinced.

But some Republican leaders it seems, stemming from the very top (I'm talking Mike Pence level), refused to acknowledge this fraud. They always submit when the left converges on a controversial or hot narrative. They yearn to throw in the towel and to surrender, to go along in hopes that they'll retain their position if they cause the least commotion. We have simply been lucky that we had these independent cases, such as the Republican observers and VoterGA, with the integrity to preserve the election results and do what the Republican party failed to. This occurrence of smaller groups vying for election integrity quickly became an emerging trend. It was soon clear that the illegality in Georgia was not an aberration.

CHAPTER 8
PART I

There are egregious examples of vote manipulation, and then there are egregious examples of vote manipulation. The scandal that surfaced at Gettysburg, Pennsylvania during the hearings of November 25th, 2020 may set a new standard for outrageous electoral behavior. According to a witness testifying to the Pennsylvania Senate, some 570,000 votes went to Joe Biden, while only 3,200 went to Donald Trump. It means Joe Biden would have received 99.4% of that huge chunk of votes. The state would have gone to Biden with that batch alone.

The news was dropped at the Gettysburg Wyndham Hotel, and at the beginning of November 25, hearings commenced at 12:25 PM and lasted nearly four hours, upon Senator Doug Mastriano's request (R-Adams, Cumberland, Franklin, and York counties). Senator Mastriano criticized what occurred and called for the resignation of Secretary of State Kathy Boockvar.

Specifically, this gem came from former army information warfare officer Ret. Col. Phil Waldren. As a member of Rudy Giuliani's team, Waldren brought considerable experience in analyzing election data fraud to the hearing. Rudy Giuliani started by asking Waldren to clarify exactly what his analytics team meant when they talked about "spike anomalies" in voting patterns.

Waldren defines them as "events where a numerical number of votes are processed in a time period that is not feasible or mechanically possible under normal circumstances." He also showed a chart with a shocking example of an apparent massive dump of votes for Joe Biden. Giuliani pressed Waldren further for clarification regarding this "injection of votes." The account reads as follows:

Waldren: "At the very beginning of the chart, where there's a circle that says, 'On Election Day,' what that indicates is there's a spike in loaded votes, 337,000 plus or minus some votes that were added in there in one big batch. So that was an anomaly in the reporting. Normally, you would expect to see a smooth curve going up, not any big spikes; that's kind of what Greg was talking about, the anomalies of loading and uploading those votes. So that big spike that occurs there is a prime indicator of fraudulent voting."

Giuliani: "And that's [a total of] 604,000 votes in 90 minutes, is that right?"

Waldren: "Correct, this is (he shows the chart here) 337,000 votes in that period of time."

Giuliani: "And when you look at this entire curve, with all these spikes, can you calculate how much of a vote that accounted for Biden, and how much for Trump?"

Waldren: "Close to 600,000. I think our figures were about 570-some-odd-thousand that all those spikes represent overtime."

Giuliani: "For Biden?"

Waldren: "Correct."

Giuliani: "And how much for Trump?"

Waldren: "I think it was a little over 3,200."

The result was nearly 570,000 votes for Joe Biden and just 3,200 for Trump, which means Joe took up a majority, 99.4%, of the ballots. This is an unheard-of outcome in any election, or at least, any honest election. Cases of 90% swoop are reserved solely for fraud, whereby deliberate clerical errors amass in thousands of misplaced votes, as we have previously pointed out. Naturally, when Waldren said the official numbers, the audience in the room gasped in shock.

This case constituted one of the most deceptive examples of documented voter fraud in the history of presidential politics across the globe. Just that interference alone erased Donald Trump's 600,000-vote lead over Joe Biden; Biden finished up winning Pennsylvania by around 70,000 votes. This electoral disaster has been completely disregarded by the mainstream press, as is the case with almost every bit of evidence I have alluded to thus far.

The only national sources that I could find reporting it were RealClearPolitics, Breitbart, and Greg Kelly of Newsmax TV. The video link that I've provided is courtesy of Right-Side Broadcasting Network, a conservative source filling a gap vacated by shameless mainstream "news" sources that avoided the hearing like the plague.

The four-hour hearing provided numerous claims. Another prime piece of evidence, according to Waldren, was that a total of 1,823,148 mail-in ballots were sent out by the Commonwealth, and yet 2,589,242 mail-in ballots were counted in the final vote tally for the state, meaning 766,000 mail-in ballots remain unaccounted for. Rudy Giuliani claimed that the 766,000 ballots "appeared from nowhere." Neither Pennsylvania's secretary of state nor its governor addressed this.

As usual, Trump's critics dismissed the hearings as a partisan spectacle, though as I have already made aware, egregious voter fraud has reportedly occurred in Michigan, Georgia, and Wisconsin. But Pennsylvania is my focus here.

Just like Georgia, Pennsylvania also had its fair share of clerical interference and observer controversy. Navy Veteran and Cyber-business poll watchers, along with Democrat poll watchers, claim poll workers fiddled with USB devices throughout the ballot counting period, subsequently adding a total of 50,000 votes for Joe Biden.

The transcript reads:

"I objected, and I said, 'this person is not being observed, he's not part of the process that I can see, and he's walking in with Baggies,' which we have pictures of, and it was submitted in our affidavits, and he was sticking these USBs into the machines.

So, I witnessed that happen over 24 times. We have multiple other witnesses, including Democrat poll watchers, and I was told the next day by the solicitors via, well actually not the solicitor but the attorney that we had secured, that they said every election they leave a couple of USBs in the voting machines that they brought back, and generally the warehouse manager comes over and puts them in.

So, and talking to U.S. Attorney General McSwain and other law enforcement officers, I found out that was not the case that generally, you know more than two is unusual. So, they denied they did it, but as of today, 47 USB cards are missing, and they're nowhere to be found.

So, I was told personally that these cards that were uploaded weren't there. I demanded they update the vote so I could see what the result was, and it was 50,000 votes.

I think as a computer scientist, an American, and a patriot, it doesn't matter who those 50,000 votes were, but I'll tell you they were for Vice President Biden. But what was shocking to me as an American, as someone who has gone to sea, gone to war, [was] that that could even happen."

The story told by a family man and U.S. veteran also had the attendees at the Pennsylvania hearing in uproar as to the sheer magnitude of the fraud that grew once again. It became clear to patriots living in swing states that they were not alone and that the innumerable cases of deception were overflowing.

The story told by truck driver Jessie Morgan of picking up a truckload of filled-out ballots in Bethpage, NY and hauling them to Harrisburg PA, after which the trailer and ballots disappeared, is one of the most concrete incidences of election fraud on record. That leaves several unanswered questions. Why hasn't Trump ordered the USPS director to chase down postal records, including records generated by the trailer's GPS tracking device showing where that trailer and its contents went? Why haven't postal inspectors and FBI agents gotten involved? At first, it was unclear if Jessie was truthful in his statement, but the courts have had evidence for months.

Here reads his statement:

"So, in total, I saw 24 gaylords or large cardboard containers of ballots loaded into my trailer. These gaylords contain plastic trays, I call them totes but 'trays' work, of ballots stacked on top of each other. All the envelopes were the same size. I could see the envelopes had handwritten return addresses, and I could even tell that one was marked registered mail; that was off to the side. They were complete ballots. I didn't think much of it at the time. At Bethpage, I was loaded with two tall gaylords that had mixed ballots bound for Lancaster. These gaylords were loaded first because they would be the last off my trailer. The remainder of the truck was loaded with complete ballots bound for Harrisburg. I then drove to Harrisburg with the ballots. Usually, I offload in one of the seven docks every day, but not on October 21st; I wasn't allowed to offload. That's different. Whenever I pull in Harrisburg, I go around, and I get to my dock, and I get unloaded, and then I roll out. Not that day, not that day. Instead, I was made to wait for roughly six hours in the yard from 9:15 AM to 3:00 PM.

This really ticked me off alright because my brother was in town. He just moved back up, and I wanted to spend some time with him. I tried to get the attention of postal workers, but no one would tell me what was going on. All this was weird. I arrived at about the same time every day. The expediter scans all my seals and bar codes, and they unload me. But when I first arrived in Harrisburg from Bethpage, everything got weird. Now that happened after waiting six hours. I went inside to figure out what was going on and was told to wait for the transportation supervisor. This was also weird. 16 months I have been doing this, and I have never talked to the transportation supervisor for the U.S. Postal Service. I talked to an expediter. I come in and I see an expediter. That's who I deal with if I have an issue. I don't deal with anyone else but the expediter. I never talked to the U.S. Postal Services transportation supervisor, let's make that clear.

I have my own transportation supervisor for the company that I work for; he's the one that gives me the details. He's the one that I listened to; I don't listen to this guy. He's the guy that would contact my boss if he needed or if something ran differently. I've never spoken with this transportation supervisor from the U.S. Postal Service, and they don't speak to people like me. He's a top guy; he's the kind of guy that would speak to my boss, not a trucker like me.

The supervisor told me to drive to Lancaster without being unloaded in Harrisburg. This made no sense to me as I knew the ballots were loaded for Harrisburg and that if I was to go to Lancaster, they would have to offload Harrisburg ballots in Lancaster to take off Lancaster stuff and put ballots back on the trailer to send that back to Harrisburg. [That] doesn't make sense. This was a real screw-up in my thinking. I wanted my ticket. So, whenever I go to a place and whenever I leave, I'll get a ticket. I'll get a ticket or a slip, whatever you want to call it.

Now it's supposed to have my trailer number on it and how much I'm loaded with and the steel number. It also has my name or who was the expeditor, so I wanted my ticket. Then because I was there for six hours, I wanted my late slip too because I want to be paid for sitting in that yard for six hours. So, I wanted a late slip for stopping at Harrisburg. Also, I wanted it because if they told me to take this load off at Lancaster, I won't pull up in Lancaster full of Harrisburg crap and be like "yeah they just told me to come here and not have a ticket because I don't want to look like I just came straight here," just to prove that I was there and so others would know I wasn't the person who screwed this up. A ticket is always provided to a driver when they arrive out of a U.S. Postal Service facility. It proves you were there. The transportation supervisor refused to give me a ticket and told me to leave. I then demanded he give me a late slip since I wanted to get paid for the time I was sitting there and waiting and waiting for them to offload me; he refused to give me that too. He was kind of rude and wouldn't explain anything to me. He just told me to go to Lancaster. I then drove to Lancaster, unhooked my trailer in its normal place, and then drove my truck to where I always park it in a nearby lot, and then I went home. The next day, it just got weirder.

As I arrived at Lancaster's U.S. Postal Service facility, I went to hook up to my trailer and my trailer was gone – not there anymore. It was 10R1440. Since I started driving that Bethpage route, I've always had trailer 10R1440. I liked that trailer; it was a nice trailer. I know you guys probably don't really know anything about truck driving or trailers or anything. What happened on October 21st was a series of unusual events that cannot be a coincidence. I know I saw ballots with return addresses filled out, thousands of them. Thousands loaded onto my trailer in New York and headed for Pennsylvania. At first, I didn't think it was a big deal. In fact, I thought it was really awesome, I really did. I was like, "sweet, I'm doing something for the presidential race. You know this is cool." But as things became weirder, I got to thinking and wondered why I was driving complete ballots from

New York to Pennsylvania. I didn't know why, so I decided to speak up, and that's what I'm doing today."

It would seem now, in retrospect, that the people of Bethpage, where Jessie Morgan left with 288,000 ballots en route to Pennsylvania, were actively looking to stop the steal and protest the events of those days. Following the electoral explosion, patriots flocked in herds outside the postal center to display their displeasure with the lack of effort that was made by law enforcement on behalf of Jessie Morgan and the Trump team.

Another patriot who had his life turned upside down through acts of honesty and dignity was Richard Hopkins. Hopkins lived in Pennsylvania and subsequently was selected as a postal worker during the election. He documented a story to the non-profit organization, Project Veritas, claiming that Erie County postmaster Robert Wisenbach, ordered postal workers to divide the mail-in ballots that arrived after November 3rd from other mail and to postmark them with an earlier date, allowing them to be included in the count. Hopkins's honest contribution to democracy by speaking out resulted in him being threatened by his superiors, interrogated by Federal Agent Russell Strasser for over four hours, and forced to recant his claim by writing an affidavit. Hopkins was denied his rights and couldn't even get a consultation from a lawyer or a copy of the affidavit he wrote. His Twitter account was also deleted in the process, making it impossible to speak out publicly. On November 10th, the Washington Post published a report making false claims that Hopkins manufactured charges and lied about the incident. The New York Times also followed with a similar story. The Washington Times published another line of propaganda declaring Hopkins denied renouncing his accusations, further putting him under political attack from left-wing voters. He said in a video posted online by a friend:

"I did not recant my statements, and I would like that the Washington Post recant their wonderful little article they decided to throw out there."

Why did Richard's superiors feel it necessary to threaten him? Why did the mainstream stories fail to align? Did all swing states experience the same irregularities in this election? Not only did the media deny Richard's statement, but the New York Times reported that they interviewed representatives from all states, and not one person mentioned that the anomalies could be election fraud. The media are charged with transmitting the truth, not warping it for their gain. Pennsylvania saw the brunt of this tyranny, with numerous citizens put under the burning spotlight for simply doing the right thing. I'll leave you with one more case featuring another patriotic Pennsylvania resident with undeniable fraud allegations, where 17,000 people attempted to vote during the election, only to be informed that their ballots had already been received by mail - ballots they did not send. A registered Democrat observer states in his video at the polling station:

"I can't believe what I'm seeing right before my eyes. This has nothing to do with Joe Biden or Donald Trump; this has to do with our democracy, and I will tell you there is corruption at the highest level in the city of Philadelphia.

I grew up in Philadelphia. I was in banking at JP Morgan for 12 years, a Major League Baseball agent since 2006, and recently I was asked by the Republican Party to be a poll watcher at the Philadelphia convention center. The first row of ballot counters, people processing and counting the ballots, the first row was about 2530 feet. After that, the machines, the rows, kept getting further and further, and this whole row went back 150 feet [or] 200 feet. But we did not have access; we could see the people closest to us about 25 feet, [and] you couldn't see what was going on unless you were Superman with X-ray vision let alone see what's going on in the back. It was coordinated where they had supervisors to answer to, and in the back, there were exit doors.

I have no idea who was there, but on the right-hand side, what caught my attention were black trash bags, which looked like piles of black trash bags. So, I was standing there, and I just couldn't believe what I was seeing. There is no transparency; there is no one there to answer questions. The people [were] taking pictures and video, and when they took the pictures and video, they were asked to delete them by the security guard. So, I wasn't the only one that took a video. However, if you look at that hall, and the set-up of the hall, obviously it looks like they're hiding something, and they don't want us to see something. So, now there is a list of the convention hall people that were not allowed in, and I was one of them. I'm not going to conspiracies, but the reality is if somebody wanted to bring ballots in that back door at the Philadelphia convention center, orchestrated, they could have done it easily."

These eyewitness accounts, affidavits, statistical impossibilities, spikes in vote counts in the middle of the night, and poll watchers being forcibly removed continued throughout Pennsylvania.

CHAPTER 8
PART II

It is, as a matter of fact, the very same data scientist that uncovered evidence of election manipulation in Arizona and Georgia who also noticed many irregularities in Pennsylvania. In a desperate attempt to reverse the findings in Pennsylvania, State Attorney General Josh Shapiro claimed that Trump was actively seeking to deduct as many votes as possible from the tallying process; as we've already concluded, those claims were unfounded.

If that statement held any kind of truth, then how do they explain the other 400,000 errors that were documented throughout that following week? How exactly did these errors come to light in the first place? How were they allowed to happen? Who lets these errors occur, and more importantly, why were they allowed to occur without the proper assessing and auditing systems in place to prevent such an outcome?

The even bigger worry for most voters is that this discovery only exacerbated their anxiety. With the knowledge that the election was not only unclean but filthy to the core, how would they find out just how compromised the vote tabulation processes had become? The bottom line for those patriots was that the election was erroneous, but now they had good reason to suspect greater levels of tampering.

The data confirm these errors, and it shouldn't matter if they were machine or human; at the end of the day, they're still errors and require a second review and thorough analysis with forensic audits to rectify the inaccuracies and ratify the official outcome. Our elected officials told us to move on, but don't these 400,000 errors deserve a more detailed and legitimate explanation?

We're now looking at a specific district within Allegheny County: District 10, which has an absentee vote ratio between Biden and Trump of 17:1. In some precincts within this district, President Trump received zero votes whereas Joe Biden accumulated thousands. The reason I draw attention to this geography is that Allegheny County as a whole was much closer to 4:1 to begin with, not 17:1 as the evidence would have us believe.

In addition, all other Allegheny districts voted 78% Biden on average while we see a staggering 93%, which simply doesn't make sense. This resulted in over 23,000 votes for Biden while Trump only received 1,300, another clear case of a one-sided affair that doesn't reflect the expected outcome of a democratic election and, rather, resembles that of a fraudulent voting system. These statistical anomalies were plotted well outside of normal distribution patterns. We've already covered the logistics and math of local and national elections, and it's clear that these outliers are indicators of foul play.

Besides the irregular vote totals within the district, Allegheny counted a regular sum of absentee votes for Biden, apart from two specific date points. If we look at Trump's vote count, the data system logs report a 145,000-vote increase followed by a vote reset or deletion where he yet again fails to reach those original absentee totals, yet our elected officials certified these results without answering questions or clarifying the results in any way. "Where did the votes go?" That was the question on everyone's mind.

It wasn't just absentee votes that log strange activity in Allegheny. Election Day votes also go negative for Donald Trump. Looking from left to right, which represents the individual timestamps when both updates were released, Trump totals increased over 20,000, which were then removed as he plummeted back down to near nothing. Again, the count continued to increase and then deducted around 1,300, then 800, then around 1,500, and eventually 1,800 votes, all in succession. In total, over 27,000 votes are removed from Trump's total in the district, which puts forth the question: why does a Pennsylvania election official in Allegheny boast about how the system is intended to block ballot observation and promote systematic errors?

Now let's observe Chester County. Before we begin, it's important to remind yourself of the incremental chart we used in earlier chapters concerning voting tallies. From left to right, each vote total update should stay flat or increase only. When you see a decrease in the chart, that means votes are being deducted for whatever reason. Auditors saw from the graphs that both absentee and Election Day votes did not follow normal incremental behavior in Chester County, as was the case in numerous other swing states. Votes should never be deducted; they should only ever be added in a normal democracy. Judging by the figures officials were given at the time, Trump lost almost 26,000 from his Election Day and nearly 50,000 from his absentee total. It was reported that he later lost another 9,000, and then over 6,000 in just a single update cycle. Again, this is something that should never occur in an additive voting process, particularly at such incredible volumes of vote deductions.

Lehigh County is another example of irregular activity within the election voting data. The county proved to be another serious example whereby the left to right trend of incremental vote totals, which should only be flat or incremental, was, in fact, heavily distorted to align with the vote deficit. Republicans say that Trump received 66,000 votes right out of the gate, which was then subtracted from within hours of being recorded. Trump then received three incremental updates to get back to over 66,000, but if the incident was some form of human error, then the totals should have been updated directly back into the value that was removed.

Why exactly were updates averaging 20,000 votes recorded, and why aren't the amounts not commensurate to the tallies that were subtracted? All these questions across the commonwealth were never given proper answers by election officials. We should also take note that one of the most shocking discoveries made in Pennsylvania was the massively obscured numbers that came out of Philadelphia, a city in which, supposedly, over 278 precincts voted 97% or more for Joe Biden. Just consider the numbers there for a second. That wasn't a typo. 97%. If you live in Philadelphia, think about what your community looks like. The people that make up your street. What is the fabric of the neighborhood? According to the election, 97% of the people that you know in Philadelphia voted for Joe Biden. That's correct. Not even a third of the people in your area voted for Trump. Just 3% of residents gave Trump their vote – according to figures we've been given. And what can the people do about it?

Critics always ask why nothing ever happens or manifests from all this evidence. "Why do your claims always end up in the trash heap?" Unfortunately for Republicans, we're at a loss on both a state level and a cultural level. For example, let's look at what we're up against in Pennsylvania. The majority of top officials in the State of Pennsylvania belong to the Democratic Party, and for newcomers to politics, you might think, "Well surely that's a good thing. Right?" Well, you'd be correct if you asked that question 30-40 years ago when the Democratic Party aimed to represent the people of the nation and the people of the commonwealth. But as the situation unfolds, the Democratic Party doesn't seem to care for democracy. Their credo isn't democracy, but division and dishonor. They leveraged their control of the executive and judicial branches to change election protocols unconstitutionally and then dismiss any investigation into serious allegations containing significant evidence.

It's clear as day to most of us. Just look at how they speak of the individuals who do not subscribe to their political ideology. These are the elected officials of Pennsylvania in their own words on their own Twitter: "Using the title 'president' before the word 'Trump' really demeans the office of the presidency." These are the words of Kathy Boockvar, former Secretary of the Commonwealth of Pennsylvania.

Pennsylvania Governor Tom Wolf also made it very clear that he had no intent to look into the cause of countless voting errors in the State of Pennsylvania. Earlier, we showed you over 400,000 errors on Election Day that make absolutely no sense. There are no answers, and there were no efforts to find those answers, and that remains so over a year after the election took place, buried beneath mounds of propaganda on Google.

Governor Tom Wolf is trying to slide everything under the rug. Why is that? Well, because Democrats see this as just a mere inconvenience. He'll have received thousands in charitable donations for keeping his mouth shut, and he'll maybe get to keep his job for a little longer. Do you think he deserves to retain his position of authority after he turned his back on his people? The Democrats claim that these bouts of evidence are frivolous and hold no merit, that the voters of a democratic nation aren't bastions of liberty but just something trivial. One of my favorite quotes from the Democratic Party goes:

"I said the other day, and I'll repeat I don't know if they need a surgeon to repair their spines or a psychiatrist to examine their heads, but something is wrong with these people that they're willing to follow Donald Trump as far as he is trying to take them."

After reading the pages of figures and testimonies, quotes and graphs, and the obscene comments made by the leadership of Pennsylvania, do you truly believe that a fair and democratic election was carried out in Pennsylvania? Do you believe that these elected officials will pursue an unbiased investigation into these findings to ensure that their constituents' votes were counted fairly and that tens of thousands of people were not disenfranchised by counting illegal votes which canceled out an equal number of legal votes? I wouldn't count on it. It's now been more than a year, and for the Democrats, the uncovering of fraudulent evidence has been nothing but conspiracy after conspiracy.

The Trump campaign attempted to discredit Pennsylvania's election results. It alleged equal protection violations, including that there was an illegal, two-tiered voting system that treated voters who submitted mail-in ballots differently than those who voted in person, devaluing in-person votes. Specifically, the lawsuit alleged that in-person voters were required to show identification while mail-in voters were not. The lawsuit sought an emergency order prohibiting defendants from certifying the results of the general election, or in the alternative, from certifying any results that include the tabulation of absentee or mail-in ballots which do not comply with the election code, or that were improperly cured.

Specifically, regarding Allegheny County, the lawsuit alleged that there, and in Philadelphia County, political party and candidate observers were not provided meaningful access to watch the canvassing process, as it was conducted in large convention centers in which the Republican observers did not have full access and were also oftentimes forcibly removed (only Democrats were allowed to observe). And while the lawsuit was lacking in terms of specific allegations of widespread traditional fraud, it did allege that at least two counties had suspected instances of mail-in ballot fraud: in Fayette County, a software error with the state's SURE system caused some voters to receive duplicate ballots; and in Luzerne County, temporary seasonal elections workers discarded nine military ballots that had been received — seven of which were cast for Trump.

Pennsylvania stands as one of the largest and most successful election coups in American history, and without it, President Trump may have kept the title of President.

CHAPTER 9

Elections in Wisconsin are overseen by over 1,800 municipalities, each one having its own voting system. They use at least two systems for standard voters and those with special needs. There are 16 different types of voting machines in use in Colorado. And, in addition to the 16 models, 813 locations hand-count most of the ballots. In some cases, officials say, voters who didn't have to use the more accessible machines still used them. The lack of information about how many people used each technology undermines the purpose of these elections. There is no reliable way to know how many people showed up at each location. In many cases, the results are released by municipalities, which are often unorganized and have a variety of formats.

The county's official tally shows that over 10,000 voters in Adams County cast their ballots in the county. However, it is not clear how many of them were in the 12 municipalities that mainly handle hand-counted ballots. Ross Hein, the Wisconsin elections official, said that the data on how many ballots were cast using different voting machines will be released after the election.

Getting reliable figures on how counties voted is not as easy as it sounds.

The easiest way to get them is by purchasing them from Atlas of U.S. Presidential Elections, which is a website that lets users search for the reports from all 50 states and the District of Columbia. Data on which machines voters used in the 2020 elections can be collected by various third parties, which also helps local officials identify which devices are used in their areas. Their data is impressive, but it's unrealistic to expect that an independent group would be able to capture the complexity of each jurisdiction. In an ideal world, states would uniformly report all of their election results in a standard format. This format would include the number of voters in each county, as well as the precincts and district where they live, but unfortunately, that isn't standard practice.

Luckily for the public, mathematics can aid greatly in determining just how truthful election processes are. As we know in most of the swing states, multiple vote dumps showed Joe Biden with a huge lead that occurred in the middle of the night during "pauses" of vote counting. Well, the same goes for Wisconsin. As America went to sleep, President Donald Trump was ahead in Wisconsin and Pennsylvania, and he had thousands of votes in both states, and to our shock, officials in Wisconsin and Michigan were not able to explain how Biden's vote increase occurred.

The results of the mail-in and early in-person return ballots predicted that the Republican Party led the Democratic Party by a wide margin. However, when the vote counts were halted as evening drew near, practically the entirety of the mail-in ballots were counted for Joe Biden. Many statistical experts noticed that random numbers in statistics can be faked. This flaw can be easily detected if the numbers are falsified as we've concluded during the coverage of each swing state. Some analysts believe that

Biden's vote totals violate Benford's Law since other candidates' tallies follow the same rules.

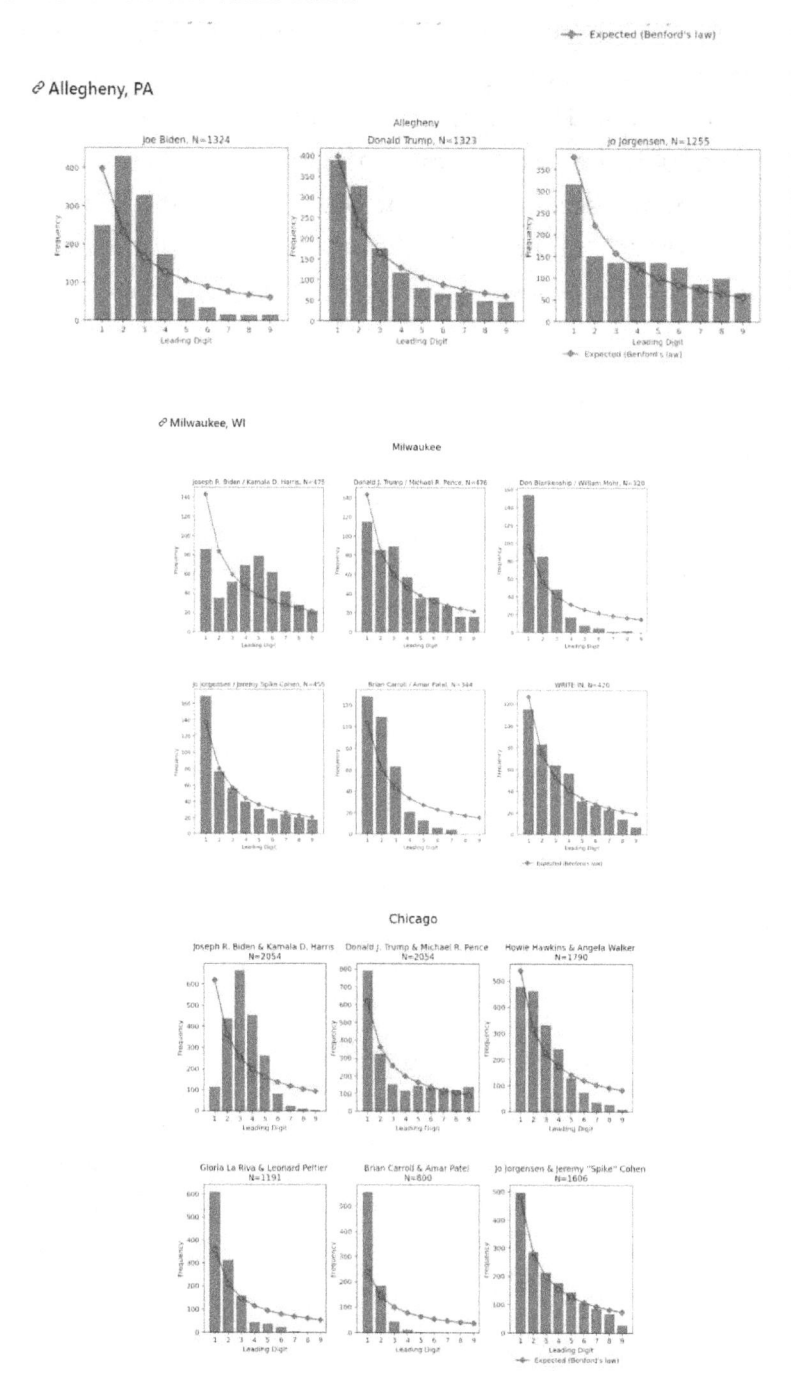

∂ Allegheny, PA

∂ Milwaukee, WI

Chicago

Analysts ran the data with Allegheny using the Mebane 2nd digit test with Trump vs Biden. Biden's numbers were questionable, but Trump's numbers showed only 2 slight deviations, and at the 5% level, they were not significant.

As an example, if the total vote count for Joe Biden is 100 in a precinct, "0" is the second digit. If the total votes were 110, then "1" would be the second digit. For Biden in Allegheny absentee ballots, there were multiple significant deviations, but for Trump, none of the deviations were significant at the 5% level.

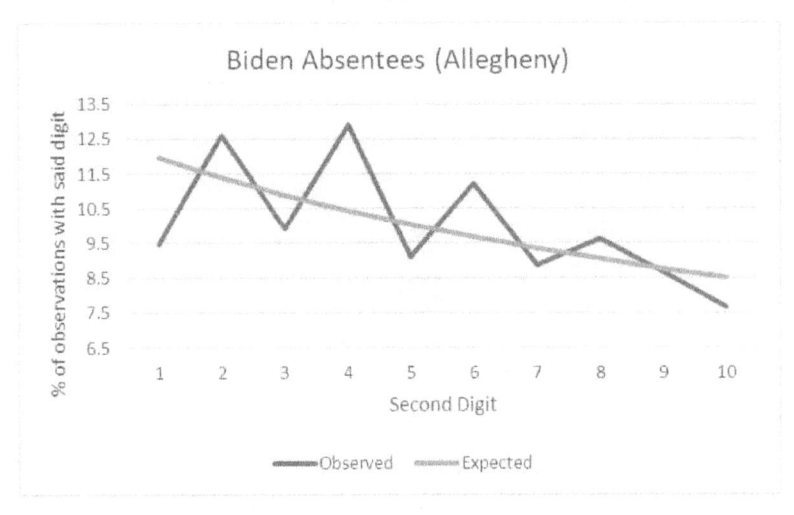

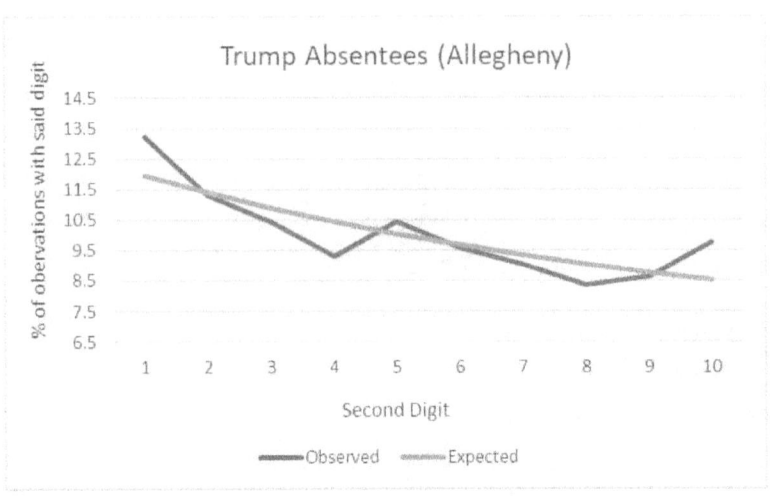

According to a report by Politico, Biden got the most votes in Pennsylvania because of the hundreds of ballots that were discovered in postal facilities, the same ballots I covered in the previous chapter. The documents also showed that Biden got the most votes in Philadelphia, which as we noted, experienced numerous voting abnormalities.

Notice also, that it is only Biden/Harris as candidates that violate Benford's Law and the expected outcomes. All other candidates, Republican or Democrat, including Trump and down-ballot Democrats, follow the expectations. Curious right? In an appeal, Trump argued that the November election in Wisconsin was unlawful. He also asked the court to order the state's Republican electors to resign. In response, the president called on Wisconsin's election officials to stop enforcing laws that he said encourage widespread voter fraud. Due to the violations of election law, Trump had the option to appeal the results of the election.

In addition to the usual petition, Trump also requested expedited consideration. A federal appeals court in November dismissed President Donald Trump's lawsuit challenging the results of the presidential election. It came following a dismissal of the Trump campaign's lawsuit over the votes in Dane and Milwaukee counties. Wisconsin voters must present a photo ID at the polls to cast an in-person vote. Absentee voters must also present a photo ID at the time they cast their ballot. The American Civil Rights Union claimed that election officials allowed thousands of voters to cast ballots without providing a photo ID or a witness statement - **illegal** votes.

In March of 2022, the illegality of the Wisconsin 2020 election took a dramatic turn when the Wisconsin Office of the Special Counsel delivered its second report on election irregularity and illegality. The results were stunning: allegations of bribery of the Wisconsin elections systems by Facebook, widespread use of ballot boxes in targeted districts violating Wisconsin law, evasion of ballot protocols to take advantage of nursing home residents, equal protection violations, and much more.

The Special Counsel report, drafted by Justice Michael Gableman, found the following:

1. Election officials' use of absentee ballot drop boxes in violation of Wis. Stat. § 6.87(4)(b)1 and § 6.855;
2. The Center for Tech and Civic Life's $8,800,000 Zuckerberg Plan Grants being run in the Cities of Milwaukee, Madison, Racine, Kenosha, and Green Bay constituting Election Bribery Under Wis. Stat. § 12.11;
3. Wisconsin Election Committee's (WEC) failing to maintain a sufficiently accurate WisVote voter database, as determined by the Legislative Audit Bureau;
4. The Cities of Milwaukee, Madison, Racine, Kenosha, and Green Bay engaging private companies in election administration in unprecedented ways, including tolerating unauthorized users and unauthorized uses of WisVote private voter data under Wisconsin Elections Commission (WEC) policies, such as sharing voter data for free that would have cost the public $12,500;
5. As the Racine County Sheriff's Office has concluded, WEC unlawfully directing the municipal clerks not to send out the legally required special voting deputies to nursing homes, resulting in many nursing homes' registered residents voting at 100% rates and many ineligible residents voting, despite a guardianship order or incapacity;
6. Unlawful voting by wards-under-guardianship left unchecked by Wisconsin election officials, where WEC failed to record that information in the State's WisVote voter database, despite its availability through the circuit courts — all in violation of the federal Help America Vote Act.

7. WEC's failure to record non-citizens in the WisVote voter database, thereby permitting non-citizens to vote, even though Wisconsin law requires citizenship to vote — all in violation of the Help America Vote Act; unlawful voting by non-citizens left unchecked by Wisconsin election officials, with WEC failing to record that information in the State's WisVote voter database; and
8. Wisconsin election officials' and WEC's violation of Federal and Wisconsin Equal Protection Clauses by failing to treat all voters the same in the same election.

Those are quite the findings from the Wisconsin Special Counsel! The cities of Milwaukee, Madison, Racine, Kenosha, and Green Bay entered into an illegal bribery scheme. These cities were known as the "Zuckerberg Five." The plot was to accept funds from a Facebook third-party, known as the Center for Tech and Civic Life (CTCL), in exchange for targeted "get out the vote" initiatives, wildly favoring democrat-controlled precincts and neglecting traditionally conservative controlled areas. The CTCL agreement facially violates the election bribery prohibition of Wis. Stat. § 12.11 because the participating cities and public officials received private money to facilitate in-person or absentee voting within such a city. This was an illegal operation in Wisconsin.

The Zuckerberg Five cities received the following amounts of money from Facebook by intermediary CTCL:
- Green Bay—$1,093,400
- Kenosha—$862,779
- Madison—$1,271,788
- Milwaukee—$2,154,500
- Racine—$942,100

For a total grant amount of over $6,000,000. These grants came with conditions to facilitate in-person and absentee ballot collections in specific locales. The grants also demanded that ballot drop boxes be placed in targeted neighborhoods under the guide of "historical inequity," when in actuality, this was designed to boost Democrat votes in specific neighborhoods, while not providing the same convenience to Republican areas. This is a clear violation of bribery law in Wisconsin as well as the equal protection clause under the Constitution. Votes captured illegally are illegal.

The report continues to state:

"Areas of the state that received grants saw statistically significant increases in turnout for Democrats. Increases in turnout were not seen for Donald Trump. This WILL report highlights the inequitable distribution of private resources that came into the state during the 2020 election. Reforms that are designed to ensure that any grant money is distributed in a per capita manner across the state will go a long way in increasing faith that our elections are being conducted openly and honestly."

Let us read between the lines here. When groups attempt to Turn Out the Vote, what they are trying to do is increase participation in favorable districts to offset gains found in unfavorable districts. This is a perfectly legal and strategically wise election activity. The idea is that a very large number of people simply do not vote – they forget or simply don't care to. Attempts to "Turn Out the Vote" try to change that calculus in specific districts through political messaging. Political campaigns attempt to create ads that encourage people to vote, and they target areas that traditionally lean their direction with these Turn Out the Vote campaigns.

Where the Zuckerberg Five became illegal was that, (1) they provided funding with conditions for general election support, and (2) part of those conditions for the money forced promoting *access* to voting in some neighborhoods while neglecting others, based on which areas were more favorable to Democrats. This is very different than political messaging. This is making it easier to vote in places that support your political ideology and making it relatively more difficult in areas that do not support your political ideology, using grant money given to the state to support the general elections applicable to all citizens, regardless of political affiliation. If you are a Democrat reading this book, imagine if Mike Lindell gave the Commonwealth of Pennsylvania $6M (now considered property of the people of Pennsylvania) to only put drop boxes in Republican counties and not democratic counties.

That is not all of what happened in Wisconsin. Justice Gableman. There was 100% voter turnout in many nursing homes in Wisconsin – where many of the residents of these nursing homes were declared mentally incompetent or otherwise ineligible for voting (such as a non-citizen). 100%+ voter turnout is impossible in nursing homes.

How did they accomplish this? The report details:

1. Residents being illegally assisted with "marking" their ballots by nursing home staff and administrators;
2. Absentee ballots for residents being illegally handled by facility staff and administrators;
3. Resident absentee ballots being illegally "witnessed" by nursing home staff and administrators;
4. Suspected forger of resident signatures by nursing home staff and administrators;
5. Improbably high voting rates for residents at nursing homes; and
6. Ballots cast by residents — where those residents were unaware of their surroundings, with whom they are speaking at any given time, or what year it is, and/or where those residents' right to vote had been taken away by court order because they had been adjudicated as mentally incompetent.

County	# of Nursing Homes Vettted	# of Registered Voters	# of Voters Nov 2020	% of Registered Voters that Voted
Milwaukee	30	1084	1084	100%
Racine	12	348	348	100%
Dane	24	723	723	100%
Kenosha	9	866	841	97%
Brown	16	280	265	95%

The Office of the Special Counsel in Wisconsin received testimony that the following occurred in the 2020 election:

- In Brown County Facility 1, 20 absentee ballots were cast. A study of the Absentee Ballot Envelopes obtained through open records request revealed all 20 of the envelopes were witnessed by the same person. At this facility, Resident A voted, and Resident A's family provided copies of that resident's signature against the signature on the absentee envelope, and they do not match. Further, Resident A does not have the mental capacity to vote as is evinced in a video interview.
- At the same facility, Resident B, according to WisVote data, voted twice, both by absentee ballot.
- In Brown County Facility 2, Resident C voted in 2020. According to family, Resident C was not of sound mind for over 10 years. This is documented in a video interview.
- In Brown County Facility 3, Resident D was taken from the facility to vote by family and guardian to Resident D's assigned polling location. Resident D had registered to vote at this location on Oct 29th as well. When Resident D presented herself to vote on Election Day, Resident D was told that she had already voted. After questioning from family, Resident D recollected that someone at the nursing home had come around talking about voting at the nursing home; however, Resident D denied voting at the home. WisVote shows her voting absentee.

- In Dane County Facility 1, Resident E, who has been adjudicated incompetent since 1972, voted in 2020. Video of Resident E shows Resident E is clearly not mentally capable of voting.
- In Dane County Facility 2, Resident F never requested an absentee ballot for the November 2020 election, yet received one. Resident F's guardian intercepted the ballot, and subsequently, Resident F did not vote. The guardian notified the nursing home that Resident F was no longer going to be voting, yet in the Spring of 2021, WisVote records reveal that Resident F voted again.
- In Kenosha Facility 1, Resident G voted absentee in the Nov 2020 election. Resident G was interviewed on video, and it shows she is clearly incapable of voting.
- In Kenosha Facility 2, Resident H voted absentee in November of 2020. Resident H's guardian reported that Resident H was incapable of voting as Resident H suffered from severe dementia. However, WisVote records indicate Resident H voted throughout the calendar year 2020.
- In Milwaukee County Facility 1, WisVote data shows 3 adjudicated incompetent voters voted in the November 2020 election. However, it was actually 2 individuals with one casting two ballots.
- In Milwaukee County Facility 2, Resident I is 104 years old and clearly incompetent. Resident I's family indicated Resident I had been incompetent for several years. This is an extremely egregious case as shown by a video of Resident I with family. Resident I cannot comprehend anything.
- In Outagamie County Facility 1, Resident J, who has been adjudicated incompetent, not only voted in the November 2020 election, but also voted in February 2021. The video of Resident J verifies the fact that Resident J is incompetent.

- In Washington County Facility 1, Resident K was found incompetent in 2018 by two separate doctors. Resident K cast a ballot in the November 2020 presidential election. Resident K passed in November of 2021.

Perhaps the most outrageous story to come out of Wisconsin deals with a special interest group operative and a hotel room. His name is Michael Spitzer Rubenstein, and his story is one of the darker chapters in American electoral history.

The OSC report states:

"The OSC learned that all machines in Green Bay were ESS machines and were connected to a secret hidden Wi-Fi access point at the Grand Hyatt hotel, which was the location used by the City of Green Bay on the day of the 2020 presidential election. The OSC discovered the Wi-Fi, machines, and ballots were controlled by a single individual who was not a government employee, but instead an agent of a special interest group operating in Wisconsin."

So one individual was hiding out at the Grand Hyatt Hotel and was controlling Green Bay's election from a computer in his room. This man is a lawyer from Brooklyn who was shuttled in as part of Facebook's takeover of the Wisconsin election. How did this individual manage to run the election from his hotel room – and why?

The report continues:

"One of the functions of Mr. Spitzer Rubenstein's service as "on-site contact" was to coordinate with the contractor staff at the Hyatt Regency and KI Convention Center to set up wireless networks for Election Day operations. At Mr. Spitzer Rubenstein's instruction, there were three Wi-Fi networks available. One was the general conference facility public network that would be available to members of the press and others. That network was password-protected, but the password was widely available. A second password-protected Wi-Fi network was created for

Central Count staff. Mr. Spitzer Rubenstein also directed that a third Wi-Fi network be established, but that network was to be hidden and not to be password-protected. Spitzer Rubenstein also ensured that "both networks reach[ed] [his] hotel room on the 8th floor. On Election Day, Spitzer Rubenstein had access to ballots and determined which ones would be counted or not counted."

Our elections can be hijacked because the electronic voting machines are hooked up to the internet. You know, the simple truth that your elected officials keep insisting is not true — but it is now established as indisputably true. This brings us to the next truth: your elected officials are lying to you, and they're probably lying to you because the only way they got elected was by using corrupt voting systems. It is illegal to connect electronic voting machines to the internet because of the threat of tampering and interception. In Wisconsin, they did it anyway and allowed the Brooklyn attorney to decide which votes would count and which would not through a process known as adjudication.

There's another blockbuster development mentioned in the report as well. The retired Wisconsin judge got his hands on some interesting evidence. The OSC's investigation discovered the use of a ballot tracking and harvesting application in Wisconsin. An extensive amount of time and effort went into this portion of the investigation. The OSC became attuned to the possibility of an application when reviewing email exchanges between the Zuckerberg 5 and third parties. This involved tracking applications in Georgia and Pennsylvania.

The OSC discovered ballot tracking programs in both Georgia and Pennsylvania. The OSC was able to locate and identify the developer of both programs in those states. The OSC obtained the source code for the Pennsylvania application.

The Democrats now have a very big problem: massive election fraud in 2020 is no longer a "conspiracy theory" — it's a fact described in great detail in an official report conducted by the state officials of Wisconsin. But it just continues from Wisconsin into Michigan and many other states.

CHAPTER 10
PART I

Over the entire duration of his presidential term, Donald Trump was the victim of a daily diet that lectured the American people on authoritarianism, how he was the second coming of Adolf Hitler, and how he would establish a fascist regime. But the unfolding of mass fraud and the coming of true authoritarianism across the nation has proven the very opposite. It is, in fact, the Democrats, such as those in Michigan and Pennsylvania, who have betrayed democracy. The majority of mainstream news outlets didn't seem interested in investigating the more credible claims of widespread domestic interference. Fact checker websites never even appeared concerned with the testimonies and instead focused on parroting what most outlets are reporting. For example, a "fact check" on the strange hidden ballot boxes and multiple runnings of those ballots coupled with the unprecedented removal of poll watchers was excused as

,"the people involved in the alleged crime said they did nothing wrong." How laughable! Soon after the election, a court ruled that Michigan Secretary of State Jocelyn Benson violated the law by altering the rules for absentee ballot applications before the 2020 election. The Michigan secretary of state, despite having the authority delegated to the state legislature, usurped the role of the state's local officials, an argument that was consistently made by Donald Trump when he contested elections in some states, including Michigan. Judge Murray ruled that Secretary of State Jocelyn Benson had violated the law when issuing guidance in October 2020 that violated the Administrative Procedures Act. State Court of Claims Judge Christopher Murray has ruled invalid Benson's guidance issued to Michigan clerks in early October that instructed them to presume the accuracy of absentee ballot signatures. Because Benson did not go through the proper rule-making process when issuing the guidance, clerks do not need to comply with it for future elections, Murray ruled.

"The presumption is found nowhere in state law," wrote Murray.

The revelation that the secretary of state in Michigan violated the law in carrying out unlawful changes to election laws is the first sign of Trump's legal vindication. However, this type of "renegade" rule-making and unconstitutional changes to existing election law by authorities lacking authority happened in every swing state Joe Biden won - fascinating.

All of the cases were dismissed without a hearing or proper evaluation of the merits. Michigan was among the states that made changes to election laws to boost mail-in voting. The Washington Examiner reported last week that as many as 28 states changed their election laws to boost mail-in voting, which favored the Democratic Party. The Michigan court case is thus one of the first serious attempts to recognize that such unilateral changes to election laws were unlawful.

Observations once again came in clutch for the Republican party during the election, as Patrick Colbeck, a former Michigan Senator and candidate for governor, released a report detailing his observations during the election. He said:

"We have heard persistent refrains from the media and complicit elected officials that 'there is no evidence of election fraud' in the 2020 election. That is simply not true. I was a poll challenger at the Detroit Absentee Voter Counting Board on election night. In addition to my own affidavits pertaining to substantive breakage in the chain of custody pertaining to vote tallies, I have read hundreds of affidavits attesting to election fraud . . . in Michigan alone. Whenever there are attempts to convey this election fraud to the general public, Big Tech censors the information or 'supplements' it with propaganda dismissive of the claims. These claims of election fraud should not be dismissed. They should be investigated in all of the battleground states as a minimum. Instead, they have been actively suppressed by elected officials in all branches of our government. If these officials truly believe there is no election fraud, why would they take such draconian measures to suppress a transparent review of these allegations? Short answer . . . because they are not interested in the truth. I am interested in the truth. That is why I have continued to investigate claims of election fraud. Upon my review of the affidavits at my disposal, I have prepared what I believe is a compelling case for the decertification of the Michigan election. The chain of custody for key election artifacts such as the qualified voter file, poll books, ballots, and vote tallies was demonstrably broken. In a criminal case, a break in the chain of custody is grounds for the dismissal of charges. In the case of an election, a break in the chain of custody is grounds for the dismissal of the election results."

In his report, he details the innumerable breaks in the chain of custody that serve as grounds for the dismissal of election outcomes. Below he lists:

"Chain of Custody Broken

- Based on the Qualified Voter File (QVF) or Voter Registration Database, 616,648 ineligible voters allowed to vote, and 12.23% of absentee voters not requesting an absentee ballotAt least 210 dead voters (Possible 1,005 additional dead voters)
- At least 317 voters casting votes in multiple states
- At least 13,248 absentee or early voters not residents of Michigan when they voted
- 2,474 voters with invalid addresses (an additional 857 unverifiable)
- Fake birthdays entered demonstrating no validation of voting age criteria being met
- Multiple versions of poll books per precinct
- Double voting due to multiple poll books
- Unsupervised ballot duplication
- Suspicious drops of "tens of thousands" of ballots
- At least 289,866 illegal votes cast
- Evidence of internet connectivity connected to electronic vote scanners (illegal)
- Evidence of fractional vote tallies (should have been impossible)
- Dominion election system's 68% error rate, resulting in a suspicious adjudication rate
- Data anomalies indicating fraud
- Statutory Violations
- Deliberate interference with duties of poll challengers
- Republican poll workers rejected access by election officials
- Election processes executed without representatives of both major political parties
- Poll workers leaving polling location before the closure of polls
- Destruction of election artifacts before the end of the 22-month archival requirement

- Interference with recount efforts
- Secretary of State Benson allowing online voter registration without signature verification
- Constitutional Violations
- Unconstitutional delegation of legislative authority to certify election results to the Governor in MCL 168.46
- Unequal protection of law provided in favor of Democrats
- Unlawful restrictions upon freedom of assembly
- Denial of access to audit
- Privatization of elections by left-leaning group Centre for Tech and Civic Life (more on this later)

Use of COVID to Subvert Election Integrity

The COVID outbreak resulted in a significant amount of fear and suffering across America.

Some of the examples of how the COVID outbreak was used to subvert the integrity of the election in Michigan are as follows:

- Unlawful 6-foot rule (rescinded by court order yet still enforced)
- 14-day extension (struck down by higher court)
- Impairment of freedom of assembly
- Stonewalling / denial of access by Detroit Elections Bureau before the election
- Limits on the number of poll challengers per building"

Patrick Colbeck would then go on to highlight that it was the same committee members who then proceeded to claim they noticed "severe weaknesses in the election system."

Subsequently, Daire Rendon, a state representative from Michigan, sent a letter to the Senate Oversight Committee after claiming that she had evidence of widespread election fraud in the state.

However, the Committee failed to act upon such evidence, an action President Donald Trump later called "a cover-up" in his bulletin:

- June 24, 2021 -

Statement by Donald J. Trump, 45th President of the United States of America

Michigan State Senators Mike Shirkey and Ed McBroom are doing everything possible to stop Voter Audits in order to hide the truth about November 3rd. The Senate "investigation" of the election is a cover up, and a method of getting out of a Forensic Audit for the examination of the Presidential contest.

Corrupt (?) politicians falsely claim there was no Voter Fraud in Michigan (has anyone looked at what is considered the most corrupt election city in the U.S., DETROIT?), however, they admit to "problems with the numbers" that rigged 7,048 votes to illegally give a very conservative county to Joe Biden, which raised big signals, only to then find that it was actually President Trump that won the county by 3,788 votes, not Biden.

The report mentions that Detroit engaged in "illegal actions" by blocking our poll workers, and concludes mailing of unsolicited ballot applications "demonstrates a clear vulnerability for fraud", and then goes on to say that no one should question this election?

Instead of doing a Forensic Audit, they want to investigate the Patriots who have fought for the truth and who are exposing a very possibly Rigged Election. The truth will come out and RINO's will pay at the polls, especially with primary voters and expected challenges. Our Country was based on Free and Fair Elections, and that's what we must have!

Call those two Senators now and get them to do the right thing, or vote them the hell out of office!

Contact: Sen. Mike Shirkey: (517) 373-5932

Contact: Sen. Ed McBroom: (517) 373-7840

Matt DePerno, an attorney general candidate at the time, claimed to have reviewed the report by publishing a response to the ordeal. In his words: "With this report, the Michigan Senate is attempting to cover up evidence of election fraud in the November 2020 general election. They are also using the mantle of government to proactively intimidate anyone from speaking out about election fraud."

Michigan was where the Democratic Party was especially repressive, and anyone who dared question the results of the 2020 presidential election was regarded as an enemy of the regime and subjected to legal and political retribution.

Michigan Attorney General Dana Nessel and state police consequently investigated these allegations that unnamed individuals were making "false claims" about the 2020 election outcome, either for personal gain or sabotage. The report stated that:

"The criminal investigation follows a nearly 8-month probe into election claims by the Senate Oversight Committee, which found no evidence of widespread systematic fraud in the Michigan election, contradicting claims by former President Donald Trump and his supporters."

But what hurt the State of Michigan the most was the fact that it was the Republican-led committee who urged Nessel, a Democrat, to scrutinize "those who have been utilizing misleading and false information about Antrim County to raise money or publicity for their own ends."

As you can expect, this was music to Nessel's ears, and she gladly carried out her investigation along with the tyrant-in-chief, Gov. Gretchen Whitmer, who together formed a legal co-op mission when it came to imposing and implementing unconstitutional COVID-19 lockdowns, business closures, and restrictions. The residents of Michigan saw clear as day that going after supporters of President Trump was too good an opportunity to pass up for Nessel, especially at the Republican party's behest.

While top Democrats claimed no substantial evidence of fraud was found, other researchers found non-circumstantial, substantial evidence that voter fraud and vote **illegality** did take place in several states, most prominently in Pennsylvania, Arizona, Wisconsin, Georgia, and of course, Michigan.

On several occasions, President Donald Trump has referred to illegal votes as the reason why he lost the 2020 election. His Twitter feed flooded timelines with claims of fraud, and his presidential bulletin makes it clear that thousands of votes in Michigan were illegally cast and tabulated. You would think that all this evidence would surely culminate in a major lawsuit and election audit, right? Well, let's look at what happened.

CHAPTER 10
PART II

The evidence of voting machines being compromised in Michigan isn't the first account we've heard that came to such a conclusion. The majority of decider states seem to be forming a trend. Not only were the voting machines constructed to conceal evidence of fraudulent tabulation, but if discovered, those liable can infer that human error was not at play and that no malcontents were involved in the switching or deduction of votes.

Similarly, Stephanie Lambert spoke about how Google software tried to stop her from sending an email to the White House regarding the 2020 election fraud. She also claimed that the Dominion voting machines were connected to the internet, contradictory to the testimony made by the Dominion CEO.

Further evidence was shown that the company and Election Source had been discussing the poor quality of internet connections at the time of the incident. It was concluded as a breach made by a contractor for Election Source.

Lambert also claimed that several Michigan election officials turned off the ballot saving feature, which was required by FOIA regulations. In retrospect, it is clear to see that they did not follow the law and prevented the images from being used.

Ed McBroom, a Republican senator from Michigan, denied evidence of voter fraud during the election. The attorney general of the state has implied that anyone who makes false claims about the results will be prosecuted.

Following the development, the campaign of President Donald Trump announced it would be filing further lawsuits to prevent the counting of ballots in Pennsylvania and Michigan, also claiming that the ballots arrived after the Election Day deadline.

This campaign was a multi-state legal fight in the states of Pennsylvania, Michigan, Arizona, Wisconsin, and others to stop a second term over Joe Biden after he led the president by 46,000 votes, with 96% of the estimated votes tallied. Both candidates remained locked in a tight race as the night progressed, but as the night came to an end, the dishonesty of the outcome prevailed.
The legal challenges were part of a strategy to invalidate the results of the election, aimed at preventing late voters from casting illegal ballots for Biden. The lawsuit, which was filed in Michigan, alleged that the Trump campaign was not allowed adequate access to areas where votes were being counted.

Stepien said that the campaign had not been granted access to certain locations to observe the counting of ballots. "We have filed suit today in the Michigan Court of Claims to halt counting until meaningful access has been granted. We also demand to review those ballots which were opened and counted while we did not have meaningful access," the statement said.

The filing also alleged that the Michigan secretary of state 's office had failed to follow a state law requiring that at least one inspector from a major political party be present at ballot counting locations, indicating that Michigan's Secretary of State Jocelyn Benson had undermined the rights of all Michigan voters. However, prior elections in Michigan were conducted in a manner that ensured the integrity of the ballot. Both parties and the public had access to the information regarding the results.

Dozens of partisan poll monitors clamored to enter as they banged on the doors and windows of the poll center, demanding that election workers halt the tally until they were present. After pandemonium ensued, Facebook tirades aired claims that Republican challengers were unlawfully barred from observing the election count.

One post cited: "The Democrats are locking us out and not letting us in to supervise the ballot counting at the TCF Centre in downtown Detroit!"

Ironically, this post was marked as part of Facebook's totalitarian efforts to combat misinformation on the platform, such as adverse statistics and anecdotes, and of course, the truth surrounding the 2020 election and the official figures. President Donald Trump repeated that claim in a speech shortly after the incident took place, saying, "our campaign has been denied access to observe any counting in Detroit." The lack of observation during the election became one of the staples of the campaign after the issue arose state-after-state.

In Pennsylvania, the Trump campaign challenged the state's election process on similar grounds. The campaign requested a halt to the count until it was clear how many votes were cast and that transparency was granted, which is the right of the voter.

Michigan law allows observers from both campaigns to monitor the count, a routine procedure during the election process. Election challengers were appointed by political parties and groups to monitor the election process. While they are allowed to question a voter's eligibility to vote, they cannot do so by hand.

The lawsuit was filed after Trump rightly stated that the vote counting process in Michigan was not accurate. In response, Jocelyn Benson, Michigan's secretary of state, warned that it would take time to count all votes in the state.

Donald Trump and his staff produced sufficient evidence of widespread problems with the election and tabulation integrity, while Democrat officials claimed the entire process had been running smoothly, even under the brunt of the pandemic.

One of Trump's primary concerns was that the counting of votes had spilled over past Election Day, and while no law exists stating that ballots be counted on a single day, counting ballots submitted after the window has closed renders the tally false. Republicans were already suspicious when they discovered that the high turnout of mail-in ballots had drastically slowed the counting process.

However, the Democrats didn't just seek to go on the defensive. It wasn't long before they launched their assault on the Trump campaign when U.S. District Judge Linda Parker charged nine attorneys associated with the Trump campaign for abusing the court system after they filed a lawsuit to challenge Michigan's election. The lawyers were faced with legal re-education and financial penalization.

After dismissing the lawsuit that sought to invalidate the results of the election in Michigan, the judge claimed the lawsuit was an attempt to deceive the public and the courts after the illegitimate declaration of victory.

She also stated, "despite the haze of confusion, commotion, and chaos, counsel intentionally attempted to create by filing this lawsuit, one thing is perfectly clear: plaintiffs' attorneys have scorned their oath, flouted the rules, and attempted to undermine the integrity of the judiciary along the way," during the introduction to her 100-page long rant.

The rebuttals to Sidney Powell's lawsuit in Michigan, which also alleged that the results of those states were manipulated by foreign and domestic actors, ultimately failed to materialize into anything resembling justice. She was subsequently chastised for this stance after the judge dismissed the suit, and even some of her legal staff began to distance themselves once they saw the outcome impending. Rather than address the merits of the lawsuits across the country, Democrat-controlled state courts dismissed the suits and then chastised the plaintiffs. So much for justice and a search for truth!Following the campaign's legal dismissal in Michigan, Powell went on to say:

"Mathematical and statistical anomalies rising to the level of impossibilities, as shown by affidavits of multiple witnesses, documentation, and expert testimony evidence this scheme across the State of Georgia. Especially egregious conduct arose in Forsyth, Paulding, Cherokee, Hall, and Barrow County. This scheme and artifice to defraud affected tens of thousands of votes in Georgia alone and 'rigged' the election in Georgia for Joe Biden."

Her team tracked the fraud to "software produced by Dominion Voting Systems Corporation," which as expected, linked directly to Smartmatic Corporation, becoming Sequoia in the United States. We already have irrefutable evidence that Smartmatic and Dominion were founded by foreign powers to ensure computerized ballot-stuffing, and vote manipulation helped candidates reach whichever tally they needed to win an election.

And based on the affidavit of a whistle-blower, the systems were designed to make ballot-stuffing immune to standardized audits. It's hard to pinpoint the exact scale of corruption that occurred in Michigan, but being another swing state with much on the line, it's well and truly obvious that foul play was at hand.

CHAPTER 11

In the State of Nevada, Trump's campaign and the state's Republican Party loudly questioned the results of the 2020 election, as was their strategy with almost every swing state. Within days of the election results, the Republican Party found over 3,000 instances of illegal voting, also discovering thousands of individuals who may have violated the law by casting a ballot after moving states.

"Our lawyers just sent a criminal referral to [U.S. Attorney General Bill] Barr regarding at least 3,062 instances of voter fraud," the Nevada Republican Party tweeted on November 5th. "We expect that number to grow substantially. Thousands of individuals have been identified who appear to have violated the law by casting ballots after they moved from NV."

The lawsuit, which was filed in U.S. District Court in Nevada, alleged that numerous irregularities affected the November election in Clark County. Clark County is, in fact, the most populous county in Nevada, and its Democratic registration rate was the highest in the state. However, the utter mismanagement of the Republican staff resulted in a weak lawsuit, which was filed on behalf of several individuals and political committees. In purpose, it sought to challenge the use of machines that enable voters to verify their identities themselves.

Trump's lawyers sent a letter to the county's counsel claiming that thousands of votes were improperly cast in Nevada. They identified 3,062 individuals who moved before the election and still cast ballots, after obtaining the list through a search of public records. They also cited a list of general election voters whose addresses were changed before sending copies of the letter to Barr, the U.S. Attorney General. Nevada's Registrar of Voters Joe Gloria said his office received several reports of potential voter fraud. The issue prompted him to investigate the complaints.

More than 90,000 ballots were returned undeliverable in Nevada's largest county, according to an analysis of data by a conservative legal group. County officials decided to mail all of the 1.3 million active voters in the area a ballot before the November election.

Clark County, Nevada moved to mail-in ballots for all its 1.3 million residents before the November election, claiming coronavirus pandemic concerns were so bad there was no other option but mail-in voting, lest we forget truckers, doctors, nurses, police officers, grocery store clerks, etc. had been showing up in public every day. Voting, however, was just "too dangerous." This is not to say some vulnerable populations could not apply for absentee status and stay home, but the mass unsolicited mailing out of ballots was bound to prove problematic.

According to the Public Interest Legal Foundation's research brief, more than 450,000 voters cast their votes through the mail-in ballots. But more than 92,000 ballots were returned by the postal service as undeliverable.

The number is based on data from February provided by Clark County Registrar Joe Gloria, who initially failed to respond.

Running up to the election, the foundation criticized such mass ballot mailings in states that were unfamiliar with the process. President J. Christian Adams said in the brief: "Mass-mail balloting is a step backward for American elections. There are millions of voter registration records with unreliable 'active' address information that will ultimately send ballots to the wrong place in a mail election,"

In total, Nevada's voters returned over 5,000 mail-ballot undeliverable in the 2012, 2014, 2016, and 2018 general elections combined. These ballots then end up in "the wild" - capable of being captured by bad agents and falsified. With the addresses and names known on the envelopes themselves and within the ballot documentation, all that needs to happen is for someone to check their preferred box.

The foundation also lambasted the H.R. 1 election reform bill passed by the Democrat-controlled House of Representatives before election night. The bill throws out state voter ID laws and allows same-day registration.

Following the discoveries, President Donald Trump said that numerous non-citizens cast ballots in Nevada during the November 3rd election, referencing findings submitted by the state's Republican Party. One of the President's messages from his Twitter account: "Just released data shows many thousands of noncitizens voted in Nevada. They are totally ineligible to vote!" The Nevada GOP noted that some of the state's registered voters had driver's licenses or ID cards despite not having a valid address. "What you may not know, is that in Nevada, legal and illegal noncitizens can hold driver's licenses and identification cards," is taken directly from the party statement. "Thus, unless they do their due diligence, they are prompted to register to vote." According to the Department of Motor Vehicles, there were over 6,000 non-US citizens and green card holders who got driver's licenses in Nevada, and over 38,000 non-US citizens who voted in the state. Why have law enforcers not obtained the proper records they needed to combat the problem? Why was this allowed to happen so blatantly?

A Trump lawyer, Jesse Binnall, noted that Trump's campaign was not allowed to investigate the extent of the voter fraud that occurred in Nevada, suppression which he claimed was illegal and a dereliction of justice.

"We were denied access to almost anything meaningful that would allow us to verify [results, including] the paper backups for the electronic machines – we were denied any access to those, except from one machine in the entire State of Nevada. We brought forensic experts all the way to Nevada – people that could have discovered this information, people that could have told us what happened with these machines, and we weren't allowed near them. We weren't allowed any forensic audit, nothing that could have given us any transparency. That's what we were denied in Nevada."

Key Allegations:

The following evidence of election fraud in Nevada was presented to the U.S. Senate Committee on Homeland Security and Governmental Affairs, Full Committee Hearing, examining irregularities in the 2020 election, c, December 16th, 2020. Jesse Binnall presented testimony and evidence that:

- Over 42,000 people voted more than once. Experts reviewed the list of actual voters, comparing it to other voters with the same name, address, and date of birth. Also caught were people using different variations of their first name.
- 1,500 dead people were detected as having voted.
- 19,000 voted in Nevada even though they didn't live in Nevada. This was discovered by data matching with the U.S. Postal Service's national change of address database, amongst other sources (taking care to exclude military voters and students).
- 8,000 voted from non-existent addresses.

- 15,000 votes came from commercial or vacant addresses (based on U.S. Postal Service's data on commercial addresses or addresses vacant for more than 90 days).
- 4,000 non-citizens voted, as determined by comparing official DMV (driver's license) records of non-citizens.
- The legal team was denied further access to perform forensic audits.

Data Recorded from Seth Kessel's Nevada Investigation:

Clark County Registration Analysis

Clark	Reg Dem	Dem %	Reg Rep	Rep %	Total Reg	Dem Party ID	Pres. Result	Pres.Margin
2000	252726	0.44931	215970	0.38396	562476	0.063346788	D+6.6%	D+25168
2004	298246	0.43583	254952	0.37257	684313	0.063266371	D+4.9%	D+26430
2008	386935	0.47406	261717	0.32105	815190	0.153009908	D+19.0%	D+113687
2012	390277	0.45818	262806	0.30853	851803	0.149648452	D+14.6%	D+100883
2016	438822	0.43094	269559	0.26471	1018301	0.16622099	D+10.7%	D+82170
2020	524228	0.40561	369752	0.28623	1291795	0.119578756	D+10.0%	D+91470

Clark County – County has shifted from D+16.62% in registration advantage to D+11.96% since 2016, a shift of 4.66% in favor of Republicans.

Larger counties can have variance in this model, but when GOP tightened registration gap by 0.4% from 2008 to 2012, they reduced Dem margin by 4.4% and 22,804 votes. Democrats expanded registration between 2012-16 by 1.66%, and independent voters gave GOP a margin gain of 3.9% and 18,713 votes. Now, even with a gain of 4.66% in registration battle, there is just a slight decrease in margin of defeat (0.7%) and a setback in margin of raw votes in defeat (9,500). Trends in favor of Republican registration should indicated a race in the 6-8% range, and a Dem vote lead in the 30,000-60,000 range.

Washoe County Registration Analysis

Washoe	Reg Dem	Dem %	Reg Rep	Rep %	Total Reg	Dem Party ID	Pres. Result	Pres.Margin
2000	68684	0.37023	83859	0.45071	166058	0.080485655	R+9.4%	R+11543
2004	83669	0.35895	101212	0.43421	233095	-0.07526116	R+4.2%	R+6704
2008	92188	0.39833	90910	0.39281	231437	0.005521921	D+12.7%	D+22791
2012	90779	0.37596	91948	0.3808	241459	-0.004841402	D+3.7%	D+2956
2016	94480	0.35857	98145	0.37248	263494	0.013909235	D+1.3%	D+2621
2020	107283	0.35065	108068	0.35322	305954	0.002565745	D+4.5%	D+11368

Washoe County – Both parties have gained substantially, with Democrats slightly outpacing Republicans in registrations, cutting the registration edge to 0.2% from 1.4%. This means Independents are instrumental to swinging margins in a larger metro area.

Results are plausible if the true nature of independent voters was aligned heavily to Biden, but the margin of defeat in raw votes is well outside the norms given the strong competition in the voter registration battle. They are several thousand over the analyst's best estimates for margin of defeat. Democrats surpassed their lost vote total by 31.58%, nearly matching the increase seen from 2004-08 when the entire state and Washoe County shifted massively (Washoe shifted 8 points in reg to Democrats).

Remaining 15 Counties

Green Counties – Totals mostly check out. Churchill gave Trump a bigger margin than 2016 in keeping with its continued movement in GOP registration. Carson City trended Democrat in registration, but both parties grew, making the Independent vote the variable in moving the margin.

Trump overperformed in Elko, Esmerelda, Eureka, Humboldt, Lincoln, and Storey from the analyst's conservative estimates for margin expansion. Nominal underperformance in Pershing and White Pine, which both yielded larger margins than 2016 in keeping with party registration trends favoring GOP.

Yellow County – Douglas County, Trump expanded margin of victory, but appears somewhat short of where expected. Perhaps nothing, perhaps something here.

Orange Counties – Massive Republican registration trends with little to no growth in Democratic voter registration. Most glaring are Lyon and Nye counties, both of which were set to deliver huge margins to Trump. They did deliver bigger margins, but not as high as expected. May want to verify type of voting machines in use.

	2020 Trump Prediction	2020 Trump Actual	Miss
Carson City	Trump +4000	Trump +3378	-622
Churchill	Trump +7000	Trump +6321	-679
Douglas	Trump +11000	Trump +10059	-941
Elko	Trump +12184	Trump +12000	184
Esmerelda	Trump +300	Trump +326	26
Eureka	Trump +750	Trump +790	40
Humboldt	Trump +4000	Trump +4188	188
Lander	Trump +2000	Trump +1702	-298
Lincoln	Trump +1700	Trump +1737	37
Lyon	Trump +13000	Trump +12038	-962
Mineral	Trump +750	Trump +594	-156
Nye	Trump +11500	Trump +10240	-1260
Pershing	Trump +1200	Trump +1184	-16
Storey	Trump +1000	Trump +1006	6
White Pine	Trump +2750	Trump +2544	-206
Total			-4659

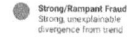

- Likely Clean — Aligns with voter registration trends, as expected
- Suspect, Likely Fraud — Moderate divergence from trend
- Strong/Rampant Fraud — Strong, unexplainable divergence from trend

NEVADA
COUNTY VOTER REGISTRATION TREND ANALYSIS

CLARK COUNTY, NV (Las Vegas)

	Reg Dem	Reg Rep	Party ID	Pres. Result	Pres. Margin
2004	298,246	254,952	D+6.4%	D+4.9%	D+26,410
2008	386,935	261,717	D+15.4%	D+19.0%	D+123,687
2012	390,277	262,806	D+15.0%	D+14.6%	D+100,883
2016	438,822	269,559	D+16.6%	D+10.7%	D+82,370
2020	524,223	369,752	D+12.0%	D+10.0%	D+91,470

WASHOE COUNTY, NV (Reno)

	Reg Dem	Reg Rep	Party ID	Pres. Result	Pres. Margin
2004	83,669	101,212	R+7.5%	R-4.2%	R+6,704
2008	92,188	90,910	D+0.5%	D+12.7%	D+22,791
2012	90,779	91,948	R+0.4%	D+3.7%	D+6,956
2016	94,480	98,145	R+1.4%	D+1.3%	D+2,621
2020	107,283	108,068	R+0.2%	D+4.5%	D+11,368

15 Remaining Counties

	2020 Trump Prediction	2020 Trump Actual	Miss
Carson City	Trump +4000	Trump +3378	-622
Churchill	Trump +7000	Trump +6321	-679
Douglas	Trump +11000	Trump +10059	-941
Elko	Trump +12184	Trump +12000	184
Esmerelda	Trump +300	Trump +326	26
Eureka	Trump +750	Trump +790	40
Humboldt	Trump +4000	Trump +4188	188
Lander	Trump +2000	Trump +1702	-298
Lincoln	Trump +1700	Trump +1737	37
Lyon	Trump +13000	Trump +12038	-962
Mineral	Trump +750	Trump +594	-156
Nye	Trump +11500	Trump +10240	-1260
Pershing	Trump +1200	Trump +1184	-16
Storey	Trump +1000	Trump +1006	6
White Pine	Trump +2750	Trump +2544	-206
Total			-4659

Various reports also alleged charities backed by Facebook CEO Mark Zuckerberg and his wife unlawfully manipulated the 2020 presidential election in multiple states, including Nevada. Through their generous donations accumulating $400 million in charitable payments to companies like The Center for Tech and Civic Life (CTCL), the money allowed the key swing states of Michigan, Pennsylvania, Arizona, Wisconsin, Georgia, Nevada, as well as Texas, North Carolina, and Virginia, to violate federal law.

It was also found that 96% of the counties that received at least $1 million from CTCL were won by Biden in 2020 after CRC traced $2,671,515 to two of Nevada's seventeen counties, accounting for 2.74 million of the state's 3 million residents. These two counties alone, Clark (centered on Las Vegas) and Washoe (centered on Reno), were the only counties won by Joe Biden and accounted for 649,980 votes, or 92.4% of his vote-tally state-wide.

The American Voters Alliance published a detailed investigative report on this issue as to how paid poll workers in one district and only minimal volunteers in Republican districts contributed to the disparity while counting the votes, which could lead to inaccurate tallies. RealClear Investigations,

InfluenceWatch, and Caesar Rodney Election Research Institute also published similar findings.

Even though the Trump campaign lost its Nevada court case, the questions it raised about Nevada's election system remain unanswered. The Nevada Supreme Court openly rejected the election appeal and dismissed it without review on the merits, even going so far as to give the Trump campaign less than three hours to submit its supplemental brief.

Naturally, Democrats acknowledged this as validation of the integrity of Nevada's election without even looking at the files that were submitted, claiming that the Trump campaign "never once presented sufficient evidence of widespread fraud." Nevada Attorney General, Aaron Ford tweeted: "Yes, they spouted nonsense in the media. But they never backed it up in court."

I heard it said that Ford's dismissal of the fraud was like a cop showing up to a bank whose vault doors are swinging wide open yet declaring nothing was stolen, and all I could do was laugh. We keep hearing that government officials need to find out what happened, not jump to conclusions based on the preferred political outcome, but why are we relying on such immoral people to determine democracy? Many of us have seen the evidence in this very book, and it's immensely concerning. This isn't about Trump winning a second term. It's about the integrity of our elections and our laws, both in 2020 and going forward - recognizing how easily and coordinated hijacks of democracy can occur through targeting illegal activity in states where there is no recourse. First, Democrat executives change election laws and protocols, then Democrat courts dismiss cases without looking at the merits or evidence. Then, of course, they say there is "nothing to see here." The Trump campaign had no choice but to go ahead and file lawsuits in Nevada against Barbara Cegavske, Nevada's Republican secretary of state, saying that the law against mail-in voting before the November election made for fertile grounds for fraud. Weeks before this, the bill was passed by both parties and signed by Governor Steve Sisolak on Monday. It allowed election officials to send out ballots to all registered voters who "were affected" by the coronavirus pandemic. This meant mass unsolicited ballot mailings.

"It will be a corrupt disaster if not ended by the Courts," the president wrote in an early morning tweet, appearing to respond to the lawsuit. "It will take months, or years, to figure out. Florida has built a great infrastructure, over years, with two great Republican Governors. Florida, send in your Ballots!" The lawsuit calls the provisions "head-scratching" since the state held primary elections in June, and the bill will change election laws so close to November.

Claims that the bill allowed ballots with odd postmark dates to be accepted for up to three days after Election Day were the focus of the attack after concerns that this bill severely heightened the chance of voter fraud and clerical error. Ultimately, Trump's campaign failed to overturn Joe Biden's victory in Nevada's presidential election.

The Nevada Supreme Court dismissed cases that sought to invalidate the results of the November election in the state, which gave Joe Biden an easy road to the presidency.

Since then, the state's Republican Party criticized the Supreme Court for its decision in the case involving President Donald Trump's campaign. They never even considered the evidence. They didn't want to be reminded of the corrupt system they were serving and the millions of people they were betraying.

CHAPTER 12
PART I

The chants of "four more years" echoed across the city of Prescott when Donald Trump's campaign entourage touched down in Arizona back in October 2020, but just one month later, a very different chant took hold of the people. Chances of victory seemed strong before November 2020, as Trump continued to campaign across the nation, asserting the deceptiveness of the polls and the falseness of the media. Republicans were ecstatic to see their president in such high spirits after 4 years of relentless abuse. However, the election outcome proved problematic for the American patriots. Nobody assumed it would be an easy victory. After all, Arizona was once a ruby-red state that any Republican candidate could rely on to strengthen their numbers. Yet recent years have proven to be somewhat troubling for the GOP.

The population has doubled in the past 3 decades, with more young people and more ethnic minorities. This influx of people from more liberal-leaning states has meant that the population has become more diverse, and thus more Democratic. But the tides haven't changed as much as the 2020 election suggests.

The media were all too quick to call the state for Joe Biden back in November 2020, which came as a shock to some viewers as they started racking up suspicions. Many onlookers gazed as the figures in Trump's favor began to diminish as the night ended, a very odd turn of events considering how much of a lead Trump had extended over the preceding hours.

And so, as has been the case with the majority of swing-states, the Trump team acted. It was months before anything meaningful came from Arizona. Trump, battling for the vote across the nation, seemed like he was running out of options. Time and time again, the courts and judges outright dismissed his claims of fraud despite stacks of evidence. Not only were the Dems fighting democracy, but the law simply did not apply to Trump for some reason.

That all changed though when the Arizona audit was confirmed back in September 2021, hoping to uncover the fraud and abuses in all of Arizona's 15 counties. After a long wait and just strands of hope remaining, the results of the months-long probe were formally announced. The news hit the ground running, and almost every liberal media outlet jumped into action trying to disparage the results. The audit uncovered many inconsistencies, including duplicate ballots, out-of-state ballots, and evidence of documents that were purged an entire day before the election.

The Arizona presidential election audit results were breaking news, yet barely any coverage took place on mainstream networks. Despite exposing thousands of voter discrepancies regarding duplicate ballots, chains of custody issues, failures to preserve data, cyber security flaws, and ballot envelopes without signatures, most U.S. citizens were kept in the dark. The audit was performed by an independent consulting firm based in Florida called Cyber

Ninjas, as a result of Arizona's GOP-led state legislature, which demanded the audit in pursuit of election integrity.

Donald Trump was ready to celebrate the outcome following the Maricopa County election audit results, subsequently slamming the mainstream media for "feeding large-scale misinformation to the public about the Arizona audit."

Remarkably, Arizona Attorney General Mark Brnovich proclaimed that he would take "all necessary actions" after receiving a letter from Republican Senate President Karen Fann, detailing the findings of the audit. The people's luck in these cases had been inconsistent, with the majority of state officials tossing any formal evidence and denigrating the party members. As has become standard, the attorney general made this statement in a tweet:

"I will take all necessary actions that are supported by the evidence and where I have legal authority," Brnovich tweeted after the audit hearing. "Arizonans deserve to have their votes accurately counted and protected."

Trump also took to Twitter, shortly before his lifetime ban, hoping to uplift demoralized Republicans after their trail of courtroom dismissals:

"Huge findings in Arizona! However, the Fake News Media is already trying to "call it" again for Biden before actually looking at the facts - just like they did in November! The audit has uncovered significant and undeniable evidence of FRAUD! Until we know how and why this happened, our elections will never be secure. This is a major criminal event and should be investigated by the attorney general immediately. The Senate's final report will be released today at 4:00 PM ET. I have heard it is far different than that being reported by the Fake News Media."

Upon the release of the results, officials were quick to point out the obvious findings that strengthened their claims. The partial draft report stated that more than 23,000 ballots were cast from individuals who left Arizona before the election. The report also showed that over 10,000 votes were carried out by individuals who cast multiple votes in multiple counties, and more than 9,000 mail-in ballots were received from voters who returned a higher number of ballots than were originally sent to them.

6.2 Finding Summary Table

#	Finding Name	Phase	Ballots Impacted	Severity
6.3.1	Mail-in Ballots Voted from Prior Address	Voter History	23,344	Critical
6.3.2	Potential Voters that voted in multiple counties	Voter History	10,342	Critical
6.4.1	More Ballots Returned by Voter Than Received	Certified Results	9,041	High
6.5.1	Official Results Does Not Match Who Voted	Certified Results	3,432	Medium
6.5.2	More Duplicates Than Original Ballots	Ballot	2,592	Medium
6.5.3	In-Person Voters Who Had Moved out of Maricopa County	Certified Results	2,382	Medium
6.5.4	Voters Moved Out-of-State During 29-Day Period Proceeding Election	Voter History	2,081	Medium
6.6.1	Votes Counted in Excess of Voters Who Voted	Certified results	836	Low
6.6.2	Voters not part of the official precinct register	Voter History	618	Low
6.6.3	Ballots Returned Not in the Final Voted File	Certified Results	527	Low
6.6.4	Duplicated ballots incorrect & missing serial numbers	Ballot	500	Low
6.6.5	Mail-In Ballot Received without Record of Being Sent	Certified Results	397	Low
6.6.6	Voters With Incomplete Names	Voter History	393	Low
6.6.7	Deceased Voters	Voter History	282	Low
6.6.8	Audit UOCAVA Count Does Not Match the EAC Count	Ballots	226	Low
6.6.9	Late Registered Voters with Counted Votes	Voter History	198	Low
6.6.10	Date of Registration Changes to Earlier Date	Voter History	194	Low
6.6.11	Duplicate Voter IDs	Voter History	186	Low
6.6.12	Multiple voters linked by AFFSEQ	Voter History	101	Low
6.6.13	Double Scanned & Counted ballots	Ballot	50	Low

It came as a huge shock to those present at the audit, to discover that Maricopa County received hundreds of thousands of invalid ballots thanks to independent canvassing. The report listed the number between 698,000 and 700,000 ballots that contained "issues," meaning that more than one issue plagued Maricopa County.

The data produced by consulting firm Cyber Ninjas and Arizona representative candidate Liz Harris, and analyzed by Gateway Pundit's co-editor Joe Hoft and mathematician Dr. Shiva, confirmed that at least 255,326 ballots weren't located on the 'Early Voting Return Files,' a file specifically showing when and how those votes were cast. Cyber Ninjas later professed that this makes certain types of audits impossible due to the mismanagement of data. Cyber Ninjas also confirmed that 86,391 of the ballots were cast by invisible voters - individuals with no related data or fingerprint matches in official government databases. Joe Hoft made it clear that "in this day and age, that seems unlikely."

Furthermore, 57,734 ballots were considered by Cyber Ninjas to be problematic, as well as 17,126 ballot envelopes found to be duplicates, 9,589 ballots having missing envelopes, and 2,580 ballots proving invalid due to the signatures on the envelopes, which was also said to be great for audits by conducting an official signature check. Conclusively, the total number of inconsistencies found in the audit involved 428,746 ballots, all of which were deemed potentially **uncountable**.

A canvass of the election revealed that over 170,104 ballots were fraudulent and/or illegal, and almost 100,000 ballots were not counted. These issues were identified by Ms. Harris' voter integrity team, who claimed that 269,493 votes were now in question.

The combined results of the canvass and the Maricopa County Election Commission's audit revealed significant issues with over 700,000 ballots, which seemed astonishing given Biden's narrow victory over Trump. In Maricopa County alone, over 50,000 voters had their ballots counted after it was discovered that many of them were illegal.

A separate investigation conducted by the Arizona Senate revealed that over 23,000 voters were incorrectly recorded after being labeled "phantom voters." It was also discovered that over 11,000 votes were not counted properly, failing to match the official canvass. Cyber Ninjas discovered that almost 80,000 votes in Arizona didn't match those of the voters. This brings to light an important question: why is it that the firm tasked with examining elections uncovered so many errors? It's almost like the Democrats wanted to keep the invalid votes "hidden" under the table.

Their report noted that almost 86,000 individuals were identified as having "no record in the database, or with the same last name at the address in the VM55 file."

It also noted that due to the complexity of the issue, they were not able to access all of the original election ballots. This is because it is very difficult to track down someone's identity if they have multiple state and federal databases. The image below is captured from Cyber Ninjas' "Maricopa County Forensic Election Audit Results Details" report.

5.7.9 NO RECORD OF VOTERS IN COMMERCIAL DATABASE — Ballots Impacted: N/A

All voters within the Final Voted File, or VM55, was cross-checked against a commercially available data source provided by Melissa[56] called Personator and 86,391 individuals were found with no record in the database for either their name, or anyone with the same last name at the address in the VM55 file. It is expected that most if not all of these individuals are in fact real people with a limited public record and commercial presence. It is highly recommended that this list be further validated with canvassing to determine what percentage of these voters represent current and valid voters.

Personator is a best-in-class identity and address validation tool. It confirms that an individual is associated with an address, indicates prior and current addresses, tracks when and where the individual moves, tracks date-of-birth and date-of-death. To accomplish this, it utilized both private and government data sources such as the US Postal Service's National Change of Address (NCOA) service, and the Social Security Administration's Master Death List.

NOTE: The following chart illustrates the percentage of voters by registered party that the Ballot Impacted number represents. This should give a rough idea on the impact to the electorate if the votes were cast by the voters and not another individual that was somehow able to cast a vote.

Party	%
Democrat Party	43.97%
Prefer Not to Declare	29.83%
Republican Party	22.21%
Independent	2.55%
Libertarian Party	1.3%
Green Party	0.12%

A total of 86,391 individuals did not have records to prove their identities. Most of them were registered as Democrats. The audit also uncovered that 73.8% of the unknown voters in the Maricopa County election were Democrat-affiliated.

If the Senate subpoenaed the VRAS servers to investigate if other issues affected the database, then we might have known a lot more, as was stated by other social commentators and outlets. Coincidentally, roughly 400,000 voter registration forms submitted during the 2020 election in Arizona were not checked against the Social Security Administration's database.

Reports and discoveries confirm what many of us suspected all along: that the 2020 election was influenced by a covert campaign of foul play and sabotage; however, officials like the attorney general could make no such claim. The numbers identified in the audit are so voluminous and staggering that few with any common sense could say this was a "typical" level of illegality and inconsistency.

1. Unobserved ballot counting

There were no observers present in the vote counting rooms in multiple counties. This issue occurred in Maricopa, Coconino, and Pima County, where counting continued after observers were told to vacate the room.

2. Many non-citizens voted in the election

Arizona Governor Doug Ducey awkwardly claimed that zero non-immigrant and non-US citizen votes were counted in the November 8th election. However, based on a conservative estimate, around 34,000 non-citizens voted, a number that could have easily been as high as 237,000 had they had access to all the data.

In Arizona alone, there were more than 20,000 "federal only voters" who failed to show proof of citizenship when they registered to vote, an occurrence that is more than double Biden's victory margin. Senator Kelly Townsend alleged that: "These voters cannot prove they are a citizen or that they even exist. They are not in the MVD system, and all they need is a bank statement (easily doctored) to get a ballot."

Key findings:

- 17,322 duplicates of early voting ballots went unreported in Maricopa County, of which 25% of duplicates arrived between Election Day and several days after, many of them with no signatures.
- Duplicate ballots had incorrect or missing serial numbers, and many contained already used serial numbers.
- More duplicate ballots than original ballots were found.
- More than 9,000 mail-in voters returned more ballots than what was initially sent.
- 397 mail-in ballots were returned with no evidence of them being sent out.

- More than 20,000 voters voted via mail-in ballots despite moving to a different location.
- 2,383 voters voted in person despite no longer living in Maricopa County.
- About 2,081 out-of-state voters were sent a presidential-only ballot.
- Roughly 5,047 voters voted in multiple counties (duplication of their vote, meaning if you vote in two different counties, you get two votes, disenfranchising someone else's vote).
- 393 of voters voted with incomplete or missing names.
- 198 individuals voted despite registering to vote after the deadline.
- Roughly 282 "potentially deceased" individuals voted in the election.

ARIZONA
"FIXING" THE VOTE

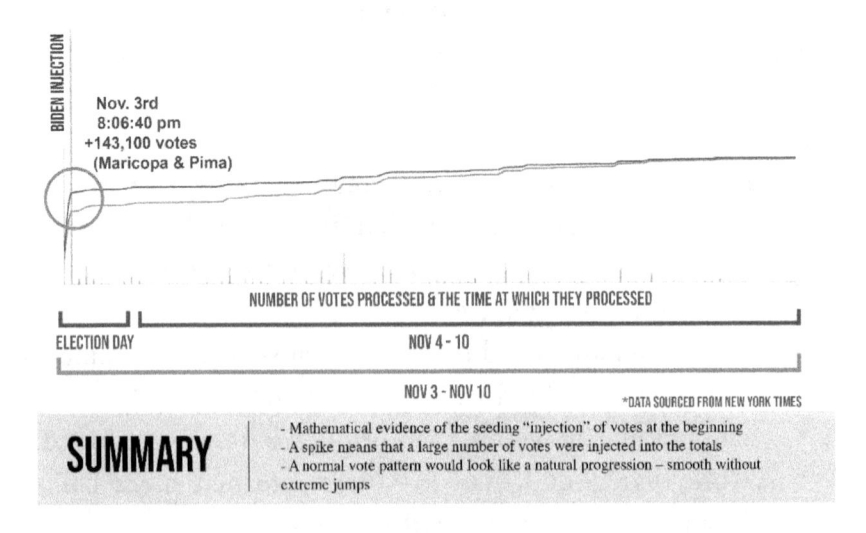

BIDEN INJECTION

Nov. 3rd
8:06:40 pm
+143,100 votes
(Maricopa & Pima)

NUMBER OF VOTES PROCESSED & THE TIME AT WHICH THEY PROCESSED

ELECTION DAY
NOV 4 - 10

NOV 3 - NOV 10

*DATA SOURCED FROM NEW YORK TIMES

SUMMARY
- Mathematical evidence of the seeding "injection" of votes at the beginning
- A spike means that a large number of votes were injected into the totals
- A normal vote pattern would look like a natural progression – smooth without extreme jumps

Seth Keshel, a U.S. military intelligence officer and statistical analyst who worked in Iraq to ensure a non-fraudulent election there post-invasion, analyzed the trends of voter registrations in comparison to the actual votes and discovered alarming anomalies in many counties. He said that the results "defy trends" that have proven reliable for over 100 years. Keshel published a myriad of reports for each county and state that indicated which counties' vote tallies line up with the trend in voter registrations and noted the discrepancies in each state and county.

Mathematician Bobby Piton examined election records and testified in the legislature hearing that he trusts that the numbers in Arizona are, in fact, fraudulent, further saying he would "stake his life on it" based on the mathematically challenging data. His estimates put the number of phantom voters between 160,000 and 400,000, lining up perfectly with the audit conducted by the third-party firm. As a result of his loyalty to his country and the truth, Piton's Twitter account was suspended following his testimony.

Since then, Trump's legal team alleged that the number of suspicious out-of-state voters was even higher than Joe Biden's margin of victory, meaning Trump would have ultimately won. The laws in Arizona state that any absentee ballot without a valid application must be discarded. As this was not done, it is clear that Arizona was one of the states most affected by corruption and political interference, resulting in a 6-figure voter problem.

CHAPTER 12
PART II

It's a real shame, and we heard about it for some time, but the nationwide audits never happened. Arizona is one of the only states where their state legislature initiated an independent audit of the balance in Maricopa County, which luckily is the biggest county in the state, meaning that it covers a great pool of voters for Arizona. The point was that people were calling for these audits for months, throughout "Stop the Steal" and right up until the inauguration and January 6th. They'd performed a few recounts here and there, but it was never what the people asked for.

What we called for over a year ago, and since then, was an independent forensic audit of the ballots in all swing states, which is completely different compared to what they've given us so far because after the election in some states, they held recounts. Well, I talked to my friends and fellow Republicans, and it just confused me. I thought, *what good is a recount? How will that determine the legitimacy of the election? Aren't they just recounting illegal ballots?*

I remember a lot of people in the media said, *well, didn't they do a recount and they found that the vote count was the same?* My thought was, *yes, obviously, that will be the case.* Nobody that I know of was even calling for a recount of the ballots because the count wasn't the problem. It was that illegal votes were counted in the first place.

We're claiming that there was a fraud on a systemic level and that the system is plagued with hundreds of thousands of fraudulent ballots where there are duplicates, the signature on the ballot not matching the signature registered to the voter, mismatched addresses or names, people that don't live in the state anymore, and ballots cast by deceased residents.

Republicans and patriots alike were talking about discrepancies with mail-in ballots, not the number of ballots that they counted. As is obvious, a recount just recounts the ballots they already have in possession. An audit checks the legitimacy of each ballot.

Last year, they did a big recount in Georgia, and Brian Kemp, the governor, made a big deal because they were getting roasted by the protesters, and they knew even back then that politically, their days were numbered. I don't even think Brian Kemp can seek re-election due to the term limits in place, but either way, they knew that Republican voters were severely displeased, and so they spent money and time on recounts.

Well, I'm not sure if they got the memo, but that's no good. As I've stated, and as you've probably heard yourself, nobody wanted that, and it turned out that, yet again, they came to the same total as the first count. Imagine my shock.

That is simply because a recount doesn't match the signatures, it doesn't check for duplicates or if they've got three or four ballots from the same voter. They're not matching names and addresses, and so consequently, of course, you're not going to find the fraud.

But they still managed to cause a scene and professed that as public officials, they did their due diligence.

That's out of the question. We never called for a recount at all. We called for, in the states of Wisconsin, Michigan, Pennsylvania, Georgia, Arizona, and Nevada, a forensic audit - an independent forensic audit of the ballots, meaning you bring in a private contractor, **NOT THE GOVERNMENT (because they have an incentive to save face for either being complicit or negligent)**.

Election officials hire contractors who act independently and who look at every ballot and every envelope and make sure that the ballot matches with the voter, that the voter cast a ballot and it matches, that you know who that person voted for, and that every ballot that was cast, specifically by mail, and specifically in those big cities, is legitimate.

Audits should also include electronic voting, software analysis, and more, but it has nothing to do with a recount of the ballots without first checking if they are indeed fraudulent. An audit was what a solid 80% of Republicans wanted last year, most of which were never answered. That was why Arizona was such a huge deal to Republicans. Arizona was one of the only states that moved forward with an independent audit of the ballots, and in turn, it gave us so many answers.

And these audits aren't cheap, so maybe that also had something to do with the logistics because Arizona had been going on for months, and they spent thousands of hours going through ballots and files. I remember reading a write-up of the report by Wendy Rogers, who's the state senator in Arizona, and she expressed how much of an undertaking the audit was.

In summary, their findings were more than enough to nullify the election results in Arizona. We've already mentioned that 57,000 plus ballots had some kind of discrepancy, but consider that the state called for Biden **before 1%** of the ballots were even received.

Do you remember that? Do you remember that on November 3rd, Fox News, early in the evening just minutes after the polls closed in Arizona, called the state for Biden with only 1% reporting in? What was so comical about that was that even the liberal mainstream networks didn't call it that early. Even they said it was soon enough to call Arizona when not nearly enough ballots had been received. It wasn't until days later that all the other networks caught up, and some retracted and put it back out while some just waited to put it out, but that's how it went down on election night.

So, just think about that outcome for a moment. What was happening behind the curtain that they'd be so certain of Arizona's win despite the audit finding so many discrepancies, especially when the final count had a difference of 11,000 votes? Biden won the state by a margin of 11,000 votes, yet we uncovered a discrepancy of 57,000 votes.

How absurd is it that the discrepancy found by Cyber Ninjas was five times higher than the margin of victory? Just to reiterate, the margin of error was five times greater than the margin of victory, and they haven't once considered recalling the result or decertifying the tabulation.

All that occurred was a series of outbursts from the mainstream media and the Democrats, and in some instances, even by fellow conservatives. We were told by the establishment that there was no evidence of fraud and that fraud on such a grand scale would simply be unfounded. The evidence isn't viable. They claimed that voter fraud is such a rarity that it would be like plucking a needle from a haystack. They won't deny the existence of fraud, though, because then they'd look foolish. Even they know that it's hard to deny any evidence of fraud on any scale. So, they parrot the same old responses. The baseless claims of insufficient evidence and the possibility of fraud when the margins are so razor-thin are simply unheard of, especially in a state like Arizona.

It's just denial at this point, which only weakens the liberal position. The Arizona audit found five times as many ballots that have discrepancies than the total margin of Biden's victory **in one state alone**, and they're still blatantly denying it. That's the definition of systemic fraud. No dignified official or individual would just recount the contest. Instead, they would decertify the results, validate the results through audits, and uphold democracy because, at this point, you can't validate or invalidate ballots through a simple recount. The election doesn't count, as far as I'm concerned, when so much error is so clearly prevalent in just a single state.

The whole point of an election is that you're supposed to take everybody that votes, count up all the votes, and then the candidate with the highest tally of votes wins. But if the margin of victory was so small and the discrepancies were so great, then the contest is void of any legitimacy - until confirmed via audit. It's crystal clear that the system is broken if such a margin of error can be produced in one of the fifty states. Whether deliberately because there was criminal conduct and foul play, or even accidentally, it's a truly broken system, which is precisely why so many people do not recognize Biden as a legitimate president. If they had any decency, they would throw out the results altogether and say that those elector votes don't go to anybody until the election process is mended.

I'd like to show you just a summary from National File (which blew my mind upon first reading it), which covered the general findings from the audit soon after the results were released. It says:

"The forensic audit of Arizona's Maricopa County revealed thousands of discrepancies and issues with EV32 and EV33 ballot forms, along with a number of other serious election integrity problems.

Doug Logan, the CEO of Cyber Ninjas, the firm who led the forensic audit of Maricopa county's 2020 election, said the results revealed serious problems with the ballot forms, voters, and other things, and as state senator Wendy Rogers noted, the number of errors discovered is far more than the 10,000 votes needed to flip the election.

Logan first explained that duplicate ballots, which are not the same as duplicated ballot envelopes, were commingled with original ballots. Many of these ballots had incorrect or missing serial numbers. However, these were small, which eventually corrected and gave a few hundred votes back to Biden as the mainstream media originally mentioned before the Senate hearing. Logan attributed these to simple human error.

He confirmed, though, the ballot form numbers did not match up. EV32 voting forms, which match with votes sent, did not match the number of EV33 forms for early votes returned. 9,041 more mail-in voters were shown as being returned than were sent out with EV32s. 397 mail-in ballots were never sent and do not have a corresponding EV32. 255,326 early votes did not have a complimentary EV33. Many issues were also seen with voters who registered as having moved.

23,344 voters voted via mail-in ballot, where nobody else of the same name was at that address, eliminating students and other people in similar family situations from the potential mix. Mail-in ballots cannot be forwarded, meaning the only legal way for these Maricopa voters to have received their ballot was to have picked it up in person, something that the audit team considered unlikely.

2,081 voters even moved out of state and received a full ballot - not a federal-only ballot, meaning they were voting in state races while not living in the state. Logan claimed that potentially up to 5,047 individuals voted in more than one county, with voters having the same names and same birth year. 393 voters also had an incomplete name. 198 voters registered after the October 18th cut-off and still voted.

Issues were also seen with the voter roll, where there were 2,681 unique AFSEQ numbers, which are supposed to be applied to voters for a singular transaction being shared between voters. The Maricopa audit team said this suggested an election integrity issue with the ballot data itself. Other claims included 282 potentially dead voters and 186 people with potential duplicate IDs.

Maricopa County attempted to fact check a number of the claims from Logan in a Twitter thread but severely ignored a significant number of points brought up in the Senate hearing, which preceded the report, including the fact that those who moved out of state should have only received a federal only ballot, but received a full ballot; the names that matched up including first, middle, and last names; voters of multiple IDs; and AFCEQ number problems.

As National File reported earlier in the presentation, Logan confirmed that Cyber Ninjas was not given key information from Maricopa County until the day before the hearing, making it impossible for the group to verify the accuracy of Maricopa county's claims.

When using signature presence detection analysis, the audit found, in excess of 9,589, votes with signatures that were either blank or were scribbles (note, scribbles are defined not just as hard to read signatures, but simply "X"s or "scratch through lines"). Photos shown in the presentation included totally blank ballots being stamped "approved." Dr. Shiva also said that the number of duplicates was closer to 27,000, not 17,000."

This was an extensive report which goes on to explain a lot of the information we've already covered. It just helps put the whole dynamic into perspective. The mainstream media never highlighted the discrepancies themselves, the missing numbers, procedures not being followed, the fact that there are obvious duplicates. If you search for articles about the Arizona audit using major search engines right now, the first 50-100 articles either cover how a couple of hundred votes were given to Biden or regard the complete falsehood which is that the audit didn't find any concrete evidence of fraud. . So, where do we go from here? What is next for American elections and the integrity of democracy?

CHAPTER 12
PART III

First and foremost, perhaps the most alarming detail that was covered in the report was the fact that many of the signatures were nothing more than scribbles, which is a serious problem because, of course, when somebody mails in a ballot, how do you verify that the person for whom that ballot was intended filled it out and sent it back? Well, just like anything else of that caliber, you match their signature. Like when somebody submits a cheque to the bank, they sign it to show who is writing the cheque.

So, the person that it's billed from actually wrote the cheque, and then the bank has a confirmation signature that they match with the one on the cheque, so the bank knows that you signed the cheque. That's exactly how mail-in ballots are supposed to work.

The system is vulnerable and one of their primary security measures is like anything else where you sign. One signs the ballot, and they can verify that when they solicit a ballot to somebody that's going to vote by mail that it was the intended person who returned it.

But for "whatever reason," Arizona received 10,000 ballots with no signatures or scribbles where the signature should be (a scribble being an "X" mark or a "dashed line" or some other "non-signature"), and that detail wasn't even in the report. We received all these findings in the final report from the independent auditor, and not to mention the fact that the data is not even reliable because Maricopa County stonewalled this process, which we already covered. In short, the county only overturned key data for the final day before the hearing.

Wendy Rogers summarised it quite well, saying that:

"We had 3,400 more ballots cast than recorded; 9,000 more mail-in ballots received and recorded than sent out; more ballots on Election Day than showed up to vote; 2,500 ballots showing an early vote returns that do not have a voter listed that is casting the ballots; [and] 255,000 early votes found in the final vote returned that do not have a corresponding entry in the early voting return file."

So, in other words, they were not recorded as being returned, but they were in the final count, and you've got a quarter of a million votes that were never recorded, which they received as an early vote, but somehow finished up counting.

23,000 people voted by mail after they moved out of state after the October 5th deadline, which stated that voting within the state after that deadline meant the vote wouldn't count. Additionally, the election in Arizona alone counted, potentially, 300 dead voters.

The president of the Arizona State Senate sent a letter to the Arizona Attorney General calling for a criminal probe into the 2020 election in Arizona, specifically in Maricopa County, which means that it wasn't just Trump and his legal team who were concerned with election integrity.

Ultimately, this was the evidence we were waiting for, not that this is in any way conclusive, simply because there are still so many problems with the data after Maricopa County failed to turn over vital information until the process was pretty much over. They certainly didn't give the auditors proper access, and they didn't supply the data in a timely fashion. There is more than enough data, however, to supply the courts with an allegation that a crime occurred. Those allegations were dismissed with no review of the merits.

Remember, this is just what we've seen. This is just what we've been able to find, and we've already established over a quarter of a million discrepancies and serious problems with at least 57,000 ballots.

57,000 ballots have major discrepancies where officials can't account for the voter that sent them, including invalid signatures or duplicates - all kinds of problems, and the margin of victory was just 11,000 votes. And here's the thing, we all know it's not just about Arizona, because you could knock Arizona off the map and Joe Biden still wins the election.

The point is this: if that's what's going on in Arizona, what happened in every other state? Probably the same thing, because these discrepancies, whether this is the result of foul play or conspiracy to rig the election, or even if we're being charitable, even if we're being as conservative as possible about speculating, even if this suggests human errors, accidents, systemic failures, it doesn't matter. Either the election was rigged, or the election system is so broken that the results aren't even reliable anymore.

If that's what's happened in Maricopa County, Arizona, you can bet it happened in Michigan, Wisconsin, Pennsylvania, and Georgia. And if it happened in all those states, you know it also likely happened in Texas, California, and probably every other state nationwide.

At this point, I don't know how people fail to understand that if these types of errors are so prevalent on such a scale, the first thing you must do is discard the results entirely. You cannot count Arizona's electoral votes for Joe Biden when the margin of error is bigger than the margin of victory. We don't know who won the election; it could have been Trump, and it could have been Biden. When you have so many errors that are wilfully neglected, how can we declare a winner?

America cannot have an election with so little between winning and losing, and then include 57,000 ballots, potentially up to 300,000, with serious problems in the final count.

You really can't count any of the ballots outside Maricopa County either because they were tabulated using the same system. It's the same system in every state; it's the same level of mail-in ballots; it's the same drop box procedure. If it's happening nationwide, who's to say that Arizona, the only state that cared to investigate this issue with this level of detail, was the only state where this problem arose?

What they now need to do is conduct a full forensic ballot audit independently in places like Milwaukee. They need to do one in Philadelphia. They need to do one in Atlanta. They need to do one in Detroit. To regain control of democracy, we need to get to the bottom of every one of these swing states, at the bare minimum.

And if we're being realists here, I'm sure millions would agree, we need a complete 50-state independent ballot audit. Start with the swing states, which is what was called for because many already suspected foul play, just not to such a degree.

We saw the shenanigans in 2020. It's quite amusing to those who can see with clarity, because objectively speaking, there's never been an election like this. That is the truth. Never in American history has there been an election when 46% of the ballots were conducted by mail. Just consider how many ballots were cast in the 2020 presidential election. The final total came to 160 million votes, and almost 80 million of those votes were submitted by mail.

I would understand if I heard people saying, *you're a sore loser. You can't let it go. It was an election like any other election, but your guy lost, and suddenly elections don't count.* The truth is that I could honestly understand that argument if that were the case, but this election was simply unprecedented in the magnitude of mail-in voting and how it was conducted, with people putting ballots in drop boxes for weeks on end, not to mention that they did not solicit these ballots but simply mass-mailed them everywhere.

These people believe that it's completely normal that for the first time, at this level, states are deploying millions of ballots to an already stretched postal service with stakes higher than many previous modern elections. Quite frankly, it's nothing but sensible to state how absurd the election process was. But forget sensibleness. The state stamps the mark of immunity on the election, even when so many ballots that were as good as gold were left unopened in mailboxes, and ballots with invalid signatures were being maliciously accepted.

One of my friends told me that his uncle, who died 20 years ago, received a ballot. His wife found the ballot in the mail, and he died before the turn of the century. Believe me, when I say, that's not an isolated incident. I've heard this story hundreds of times. My point is if deceased people are getting ballots, and ballots are just being dumped in drop boxes or submitted through the post office in mailboxes without signatures, who is even voting? We've already covered this in numerous states, and that was discovered without the need for an audit. So, just imagine what we would uncover if a proper audit, like the one in Arizona, was conducted nationwide.

We have no idea who these people are, and we don't even know if the ballots that arise in the mailboxes are even remotely legitimate. We know they "forget" to check for signatures or duplicates. We know that the election officials were deceitful in their conduct in more than just one state. We know that they tried and succeeded to insert more ballots into the system than were valid. We know they tried to steal and transfer votes through supply chains and clerical methods. There has never been an election like this, ever.

Yet the Democrats continued their parade of insults and ignorance. It was always the same flawed statement: *2016 was stolen; 2020 was the most secure election ever! You lost, and now you say that it was because there were fraudulent ballots on a scale unprecedented in history in five states?*

Well, yes! You know what, probably significantly more - in fact, probably every state because never has an election been conducted like this. In many European countries, democracies don't even allow ballots to be sent through the mail, like France for example. The French government claims that mail-in voting is not secure enough, and before this election, U.S. mail-in ballots were thought of in the same way. Mail-in ballots were hard to come by, and the practice wasn't encouraged; instead, a process called absentee ballots were preferred for those out of town or too sick to vote in person. They never gave out 100 million mail-in ballots before, and in states like Wisconsin, they modified their laws.

In Wisconsin, if you had an indefinitely confined status confirmed (such as imprisonment or any other extenuating circumstances making you unable to leave the house), you could receive a mail-in ballot. So, naturally, they were only granted to a select amount of people with very little identifying information. But as we all know, the timing of the pandemic expanded that process to virtually everybody - and perhaps illegitimately. Did the entire country need to vote by mail because of a disease with a 99.9% survival rate for those under 65? Why not just have mail-in ballots for those older or infirm? As you now know, that was the plan altogether.

I'm sure the more digging that you do and the more states that are audited, the more of this that you will find. A bit of retrospection makes you realize how ridiculous this country has become. All people were asking for was honesty.

I remember watching the results until 2:00 AM, and the networks and news outlets announced that they stopped counting. I also remember that in Pennsylvania, Georgia, Wisconsin, and Michigan, President Trump had a lead that was so big, they said it was mathematically insurmountable; I remember that. Mathematically, outlets and bookies said it would have been virtually impossible for Biden to overcome Trump's lead in Michigan, Wisconsin, and Georgia, and then they stopped counting the ballots. Then the vote spikes at 3:00 AM and 4:00 AM (when apparently, they had stopped counting), virtually all for Joe Biden.

They said Trump had over an 80% chance of winning in those select states, making him the president. It should have been virtually impossible for Biden to claim victory - until they halted the counting.

We mentioned it in earlier chapters. They told the tabulators to go home, and they stopped updating the polls on all the websites and in the news media. Everybody went to bed. I remember vividly watching the results for two hours, and they didn't budge an inch. The vote tally in Pennsylvania didn't add a single vote after a certain point in the evening, the same with Wisconsin, Michigan, Georgia, Arizona, and Nevada.

But lo and behold, counting magically resumed just a few hours later, and that's when they started dumping ballots in Milwaukee, and Wisconsin flipped. Then they dumped all the ballots in Detroit, and Michigan flipped. And weeks later, after they'd found enough ballots to challenge Trump, Georgia flipped, and subsequently, Joe Biden was declared the victor as the presumptive president-elect. All of it happened around 3:00-4:00 AM - the infamous, statistically impossible "vote spikes" that form the cover of this book.

They even went as low as to put up cardboard pizza boxes in the windows of the Detroit voting center to thwart journalists and patriots observing the count. So, this is what we're left with. Without an independent audit of the ballots in every swing state, not only will the people not decertify the result, but it won't give any credence to further elections because the creases in the process were never ironed out. The audit won't decertify the Joe Biden presidency, but it will destroy what little credibility the Democratic Party has left, and hopefully, it will serve as an impetus for serious election reform. Democracy cannot prevail if that is the case. We can never have a fair election or place our confidence in the results if this continues.

Especially in a representative democratic republic, all the heads of state, and the congressmen, and the people that make the laws should possess integrity; when they're all decided by elections, it's vital that those elections possess integrity. Tens of thousands of errors, illegal votes, aberrations, and what have you in every state - democracy cannot survive under such a situation.

As citizens of this country, and after seeing the audit results in Arizona, we must pass election reform. Only when that happens can we consider voting confidently in future elections.

However, as far as I'm concerned, the 2020 election was completely illegitimate. It's been proven simply by the data uncovered in Arizona. The State of Wisconsin needs to consider conducting an independent audit, as do Michigan, Georgia, and Pennsylvania because they all have Republican state legislatures. Republicans need to begin demanding that these legislatures act regarding forensic audits and use their votes as leverage, or else Republicans will begin losing more frequently and more severely. And when Democrat-controlled courts attempt to block these investigations and audits, keep pushing with additional legislation.

CHAPTER 13

The conflict surrounding the election in North Carolina blossomed back in August 2020. The two political parties sued to prevent North Carolina's election officials from enforcing rules that could affect the number of votes counted within the state. The lawsuit claimed that a new system for handling late absentee ballots would subsequently allow voters to cast their ballots without valid witnesses or proper verification.

The election board's new guidance, like other states, actually allowed voters to fix defective mail-in absentee ballots without requiring them to complete a new ballot. Absentee voters who provided incomplete information about their envelopes when dropping off their ballots won't have to do so again. The election officials could "do it for them."

As of now, North Carolina remains one of the eight states with notary witness requirements concerning absentee ballots. The General Assembly leaders also sued the State Board of Elections and Ethics Enforcement. They accused the board members of illegally altering the rules for absentee ballots. One of the primary lawsuits, which was filed by the Republican National Committee, sought to oust the elections board as acting in a partisan manner when it issued guidance that undermines a law designed to prevent fraudulent balloting.

In line with the constitution and Western democracy, the suit argued that allowing people to vote during the outbreak undermines safeguards designed to ensure that the upcoming election is secure and fair, thus the Trump campaign and the Republican National Committee sued the Board of Elections, claiming it was attempting to count late-arriving ballots and shift the election in the Dem's favor, and that Circosta and other officials violated the state's open meeting law by suppressing public records.

Naturally, the lawsuit delegated Damon Circosta, the chairman of the North Carolina State Board of Elections, as the primary defendant, as well as several congressmen and a couple of state officials, though Circosta failed to immediately respond to those seeking comments regarding the charges. And although the claims were in the best interests of democracy and the constitution, it should be noted that, at the time, many states were expecting a surge in voters wanting to cast a ballot due to the COVID-19 pandemic. In North Carolina alone, more than a million people requested an absentee ballot.

The board's guidance, which became effective before the 2020 election, allowed witnesses to provide a sworn statement if they failed to provide an address or sign an affidavit when receiving an absentee ballot.

Dems proceeded to claim that African-American voters were disproportionately affected by the lack of witness information on mailed-in ballots, resulting in 43% of those with incomplete witness information being African-American voters. North Carolina officials accepted late ballots until November 12 and established drop-off stations for those who need to vote by mail. To understand completely, because allegedly African-American voters had "more difficulty" in providing witness statements/ information, the counting of ballots ignored this requirement under the guise of "equity." Meaning, illegal votes were counted, regardless of if there was a racial connotation or not.

These legal actions weren't simply austerity measures to help the disenfranchised; the Democratic Party also sought to pass measures in Pennsylvania, Michigan, and Nevada that were designed to steal the election, using the coronavirus as an excuse to manipulate ballot tallies and steal votes.

The outline of North Carolina's guidance and consent decree agreed and reads as follows:

• Count ALL ballots postmarked by Election Day and received by 11/12 – a whopping 9 days after the election! Postmarks were often backdated when received during the 9-day period (illegal).

• Allow voters to correct their rejected mail ballots.

• Establish ballot drop-off stations (used in ballot harvesting schemes, which are also illegal).

Coincidentally, ballot harvesting is illegal in most states, and for good reason, as anybody can submit a ballot for a prospective voter without ID and chain of custody. The way Republicans react has almost been trained whenever they hear the words "ballot harvesting allowed" because they know what it means. And now, over a year later, Democrats blatantly stole the 2020 election in North Carolina, and most Republicans were caught with their pants down.

Even when Trump was leading in the polls, the results didn't matter. Instead, the Republican party watched on as ballots were permitted to be illegally harvested during, arguably, the most important election in modern times.

Thousands of NC citizens will relay a lot of fishy information that was unearthed just after November 4th, 2020. Back in June of that year, the state's General Assembly passed a bill that would allow voters to request and receive absentee ballots even though the practice has been largely looked down upon for most U.S.

elections. Yet because of the COVID situation, Republicans let it slide.

Later that year, N.C. Board of Elections, as well as other political groups, openly conspired to alter voting laws at the last minute. Plenty of information surrounding this issue was available in the North State Journal.

One of the figures who spearheaded this charge was Marc Elias, a corrupt liberal lawyer who was leading the Democratic Party in their lawsuits against the states, ultimately trying to overturn the results of the elections in swing states. Unfortunately for those who tried to counter the suit at the time, the two members of the Board of Elections agreed to a settlement that would allow ballot harvesting without requiring witnesses to sign and extended the time to count votes to 9 days after the election. The Board of Elections tried to dispute the claims of the other partisan, but the settlement stood.

Following the ordeal, two Republican members of the board resigned after accusing the Democratic attorney general of hiding important details about the settlement. One of them, Ken Raymond, said he withheld information about the deal. The members also revealed that the office of Green Party presidential candidate Jill Stein falsely asserted that a settlement would permit the Board of Elections to conduct the election in a non-chaotic manner. The Republican board members claimed that Attorney General Roy Stein deceived them by failing to relay the truth about the ballot changes sought by the Democratic plaintiffs.

Attorney General Stein later insisted that the controversy was nothing more than 'political theatre at its most destructive.' He went on to say that: "The scheme strikes at the very heart of our elective process. The elimination of absentee ballot fraud protections in the Democrats' corrupt and collusive settlement is part of a long-term effort already rejected by a near-unanimous legislature, a federal judge, and a three-judge state court panel. Why did the Democrats concoct this performance in secret?"

The Board of Elections and the Democrats tried to enact these policies numerous times; however, their efforts were always thwarted. In an attempt to bypass these hurdles, they resorted to deception to secure a settlement that would consent to duplicate absentee ballot fraud.

Some of the pivotal moments leading up to the election can be closely linked to the failure of democracy and the changes that were made for the Democrats to achieve a victory.

One of the fundamental changes occurred the same year when Brinson Bell requested that the government remove the witness signature requirement for absentee ballots, which were later altered under the pandemic and lockdown rules.

In exchange for the Board of Elections changing its rules, Brinson Bell and the Democrats covertly agreed to modify the way elections were conducted across the board.

A statement from Lynn Bernstein, founder of Transparent Elections in NC, consolidated these claims as a first-hand witness. Similar to other first-hand claims made by other observers, it went on about how the election was conducted was completely ridiculous. She said:

"For the 2020 primary election, I was the lead observer for the Wake County Democratic Party and was deeply troubled by what I observed: a lack of transparency, lax security measures, no bi-partisan chain of custody of some critical election materials, election results being prematurely revealed, no legislative oversight, illegal processing of absentee ballots, weak post-election (self) audits, and the list goes on. After going through every oversight channel I could think of and getting nowhere, I went public about what I saw and was swiftly fired from being an observer for my party — I do not regret being a whistle-blower. My observations for the 2020 primary election do not include my county's processes on election night because the Wake election director would not allow the public to enter the building despite there being a quorum of Board of Elections members present on election night. We were threatened with arrest if we did not leave the property immediately! This is another egregious violation of state law.

NC continues to engage in illegal and ill-advised practices and will continue doing so unless the public starts to take notice and demand meaningful observation and evidence. Many of the Election Assistance Commission (EAC) and National Conference of State Legislators (NCSL) recommended best practices are not followed by counties and should be explicitly mandated by NC law. A failure to mandate adherence puts the state and counties in legal jeopardy, as candidates could convincingly claim that there was ample opportunity for fraud.

Finally, NC must stop violating federal law by destroying ballot images. The ballot images cast vote records, and a list of voter records (along with the metadata) should be released to the public along with all other election evidence. Our democracy depends on a transparent, secure, and publicly verified process."

Transparent Elections North Carolina remained a nonpartisan voluntary group that sought to ensure elections in the State of North Carolina were more transparent and secure. Yet their findings and affidavits claim the same as every other firsthand account across the various swing states.

Maintaining his form as an auditor, former U.S. intelligence officer Seth Keshel (the one who ensured accurate elections in post-invasion Iraq) unearthed several counties that flouted certain developments in the number of registrations compared to the actual number of votes.

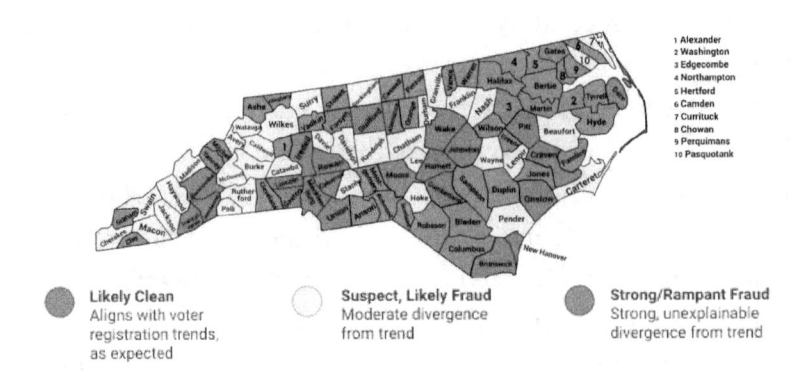

[Map of North Carolina counties with fraud classification]

Legend:
- Likely Clean — Aligns with voter registration trends, as expected
- Suspect, Likely Fraud — Moderate divergence from trend
- Strong/Rampant Fraud — Strong, unexplainable divergence from trend

County index:
1. Alexander
2. Washington
3. Edgecombe
4. Northampton
5. Hertford
6. Camden
7. Currituck
8. Chowan
9. Perquimans
10. Pasquotank

Without a forensic audit, Keshel already estimated that, potentially, 257,000 votes more than the total number of votes needed to win the presidency were counted for Biden, numbers that should have been investigated for evidence of fraud. We also know that Verified Voting maintained an updated list of the locations where their voting equipment was in use in the U.S., alongside a database containing photographs of the various models.

	Trump votes	Biden votes	Other votes
Officially reported results	2,758,775 (49.93%)	2,684,292 (48.59%)	81,761 (1.48%)
Estimate of potential fraud		257,000 (4.7%)	
Estimate of actual result (with fraud removed)	2,758,775 (52.4%)	2,427,292 (46.1%)	81,761 (1.6%)

The knowledge that voting machines have introduced countless vulnerabilities and avenues for manipulation in elections is no longer uncommon. Many cybersecurity experts profess that fully secure computer systems are nothing but myths and that the complex voting systems and election systems only make it easier for nation-state-level threats to infiltrate those systems on multiple fronts. Anyone with an ounce of common sense and a respect for democracy can tell you that the efficiency gains provided by these modern machines don't outweigh the complete loss of security, accountability, and transparency.

Such issues like barcode transparency must become a regular part of public discourse leading up to elections, or else rampant fraud will continue to plague our elections, whether they be state-level or nationwide. Citizens of Mecklenburg, Jackson, Cherokee, Davidson, Warren, and Perquimans Counties weren't even permitted to submit hand-marked paper ballots (HMPB) yet were required to use one of the "highly efficient" ExpressVote machines to cast their votes, printing the vote in English as well as in the format of a barcode. However, the DS200 and DS450/DS850 machines only count the barcode, completely disregarding the accompanying English text. But do not fret, citizens. We were well assured that voting systems used in the state were certified by the Election Assistance Commission and the State Board of Elections. There is nothing to fear. You shouldn't be worried that most counties in North Carolina still incorporate this voting method during elections and that it is still legal to transmit results using this compromised system.

The very same version of election methods that Wake County used was also used in other counties and that NC still relies on for the outcome of elections. I don't know how many people are aware of this, but when counties acquired DS200s, the wired modems were part of the order. This was completely legal at the time, yet since then, the practice has been banned. So, why does NC still endorse this process? Why hasn't it been abolished along with the 2020 election tally? We already know why.

CHAPTER 14

These deep-seated problems with election v1oting stem much further back than 2020. We've already covered so much of the Dominion voting machines and how they can potentially be used to sway elections either way. We've also covered a few instances where concrete evidence was brought to the stand, backed by real footage and countless testimonies, yet nothing ever came of it in the courts, something else we've covered extensively.

So, let's look at one of the primary investigations into the issues linked to Dominion, which did reach a Senate committee following an audit of the election. One of the major warning signs regarding Dominion arose back in 2017 when it was revealed that a federal judge in Georgia sealed a particular report from a renowned cyber security expert, University of Michigan Professor J. Alex Halderman, who conclusively demonstrated that the Dominion Voting Systems machines used across sixteen U.S. states were "vulnerable to attack" from foreign and domestic organizations and individuals. Halderman had already spent a decade of his life studying electronic voting machines and delivered an explosive analysis regarding the potential for cyberattacks that had the potential to shift election outcomes. He said during the hearing in 2017 that:

"I know America's voting machines are vulnerable because my colleagues and I have hacked them repeatedly, as part of a decade of research studying the technology that operates elections and learning how to make it stronger. This puts the entire nation at risk."

Professor Halderman was questioned by Senator Risch, who wanted clarification as to whether the machines required a connection to the internet. Halderman assured him that the machines themselves never need a direct connection for remote attacks to occur. He professed that the only link attackers need comes from the IT equipment in election offices.

On September 21st, 2021, Halderman filed a motion with the Georgia federal court pleading that they unseal his 25,000-word cyber report on Dominion voting machines. The cyber report, now concealed from the public, was presented as evidence in a concurrent civil case, which sought the elimination of Dominion voting machines from all election processes in the State of Georgia. According to his sworn declaration, Halderman details the vulnerability Dominion's voting machines pose to election integrity, stating that the malware risk is "urgent" and that the report must be delivered to the Cybersecurity and Infrastructure Security Agency (CISA) to prevent such threats. Professor Halderman's statement reads as follows:

"Informing responsible parties about the Dominion ICX's vulnerabilities is becoming more urgent by the day. Foreign or domestic adversaries that you will support, who are intent on attacking elections, certainly could have already discovered the same problems I did. It is important to recognize the possibility that nefarious actors have already discovered the same problems I detailed in my report and are preparing to exploit them in elections."

Recently endorsed by Donald Trump, Matt DePerno was the first attorney in America to have a court order to audit the Dominion machines. DePerno held a press conference that sought to highlight the findings of the audit, yet only two reporters attended the conference through media censorship.

DePerno uncovered key information in his investigation into the forensic images on the Dominion voting system, findings he wanted to display by holding a press conference to let people hear about the issues directly, allowing the media to listen to this information and ask questions. However, the majority of DePerno's findings in Michigan, everything he's discovered, has been completely overlooked by the mainstream media there.

Unfortunately for hard-working patriots like DePerno, the MSM continued to ignore his efforts to bring key evidence to light in a formal and democratic procedure. His aim to invite them on location, affording them the freedom to question the findings rather than simply write articles, was shunned. You would assume from a logical standpoint that they would be desperate to show up to at least try to embarrass DePerno and the proceeding, similar to what they did to President Donald Trump by bombarding him with questions. But that wasn't the case.

DePerno even suggested after the hearing was over that the low turnout proved reporters were simply fearful of what he had to say and what they would see once they watched the videos because then they'd have to acknowledge the data. There is no way you can refute it once you've seen the findings. If they acknowledge the audit, that means they must write about it, and then people will read about it.

This, of course, we know by now, is intentional. We understand that it's intentional. They don't want to hear the truth, and it is willful ignorance on their part. Our media has plummeted to a position where they cannot even engage in true journalism or engage in a discussion with people about one of the most important issues that came out of 2020-2021 in America. One of the 2 reports who cared to attend the hearing wrote in her article: "DePerno dropped a bombshell when he explained that he and his investigators have allegedly figured out how 'anyone who has access to the election tabulator' can 'reopen the election, run more ballots through the tabulator, print off a new tabulator tape with the new ballots, and backdate that tape to November 3rd. If counting canvassers in Michigan matched the number of votes on the tabular tape compared to the poll books' matches, they would have certified significant potential for fraud exists with these machines."

In other words, once the election is over, in the middle of the night, everything is halted and the election officials double run the ballots through the machines, leaving people on the 4th of November wondering how more ballots backdated to November 3rd were run through the machines. Half of the country woke to the news that officials found all these extra ballots, not through any legitimate cause. **Simply put, they ran through a lot of the same ballots two or three times** like they did in Georgia- on videotape and using Dominion voting machines. That's what you must understand, and that's what I've covered so far in almost every chapter.

When you close out an election, let's say at 8:00 PM on election night, as the clerk for the precinct, this means you put your key fob on the machine, turn it, and the election is over. Once that happens, that particular machine prints out a tabulator tape, and it tells us how many votes each candidate received. That's an election record, and it must be kept under federal law for at least 22 months.

So, what happens if your candidate is not winning at that point? Well, in many cases across the nation, at 2:00 AM, officials went back to their machines after everyone had cleared the counting facility. They then put their key fobs back in their machines to reopen the election and stuffed them full of ballots one after the other, as many as they needed to close that gap.

They continued that on through the night, into the morning, and throughout the day, all while the news media reported that they were still counting. However, just 2-3 days later, you can close that election again, reprint that tape, and put November 3rd as the date. That essentially creates a phantom paper trail. It's also important to note that as well as disposing of the tape, claiming these new election results showing your candidate having won as valid is a serious offense.

"Fact Checkers" have tried to claim that these are "clerical errors" or that "an extra zero was put on accidentally, but it was corrected," but when you see spikes of votes late at night when counting is supposedly "closed," and the spikes go 100% to Biden and 0% to Trump, this stretches plausibility. To use the adage, what is the simpler explanation - that every swing state Joe Biden won, in the dead of night, all had the same ballot spikes when counting was supposedly paused, and virtually every ballot collected went for Biden? Is it a simpler explanation that this was some miraculous series of coincidences on the level of the second coming of serendipitous luck? Or was it, as the Times article put it, a "vast cabal conspired to 'fortify' the election" to ensure Donald Trump did not win? This is where the famous meme below comes from:

FRAUD

The above pattern is so statistically impossible in a single case, and then to be replicated many times in every swing state Biden won - the changes of that are astronomically unlikely.

What is so devious and so fraudulent is that no one is ever going to be able to match up the ballots to that tape because now neither DePerno nor independent auditors can look at those ballots and definitively say what the correct number is. This was one of the primary ways in which fraud occurred using the Dominion machines. Another way they prevented auditors from looking at ballot count was by discarding digital records far before it was legally allowed. DePerno reported that this is what happened in Michigan.

Officials are required to keep a digital record for 22 months, so when you feed in that ballot, the machine should take the picture. As a state official, you report that the machine took the picture, yet the 83 county clerks in Michigan turned off their devices that stored the images.

The machines took the pictures as usual but did not store the picture afterward, therefore, you cannot properly audit how many times each ballot was passed through the machine. DePerno even collected emails from the clerks across the State of Michigan in response to a Freedom of Information act request they received in July of 2020.

Every clerk received the same request, and they collectively decided that the best thing to do would be to turn off the function on the tabulator across the state. Not just in one county – across the entire state. Regardless of which machine you use, they all function the same. If anyone turned that feature off that saves the ballot image, that goes against the default function, which is to capture the image and save it. This required an intentional act.

So, we know someone intentionally flicked a switch, and by turning it off, they deleted that image (this is against federal law). All they must do then is respond to the FOIA requests by claiming that they no longer have this digital information on hand. Thanks to the Michigan investigation, we even know who spearheaded the operation to thwart the Trump presidency. Ironically, it was a Republican clerk out of Ottawa County named Justin Roebuck. This was a Republican. He spearheaded this operation in Michigan to shut down the ability of voters. Many believe those who were involved were operating in a RICO violation capacity (essentially conspiring the timing and efforts across state lines to commit a crime).

When people talk about conspiracy, Republicans have had access to evidence of criminal conspiracy for a long time. This isn't a fantasy. It's all information obtained from the secretary of state, showing that Michigan clerks talked about deleting records on the Dominion machines.

The secretary of state in Michigan, Jocelyn Benson, was required under Michigan statute to keep the Dominion source code in trust. Of course, it wasn't just Dominion, but Dominion is the primary focus. As secretary of state, she was supposed to keep that source code protected. Not only did she fail to do this, but the advisory opinions to that statute also claim that she should have performed source code security audits or penetration testing frequently, at a minimum, annually. This was her sworn duty as the secretary of state in Michigan, the highest-ranking elected official in the state who oversaw the election in 2020, and she completely failed in this respect. When the auditors questioned her performance in this area, they soon discovered that she had not been performing source code audits or penetration testing, and when confronted with this fact, she directed the auditors somewhere else. However, the state of affairs gets even sadder.

Auditors also asked Benson to explain, in three separate stages, how the Dominion voting systems worked. To their shock, she responded with a declaration of ignorance and suggested that the auditors ask the manufacturer for such information. Remember that back in December, the secretary of state came out publicly and declared what transpired in Antrim County was nothing more than human error and that this was the safest election in the history of the country, not just Michigan.

In retrospect, how could she make a statement like that on December 14th after admitting to the public that she knows nothing about how these machines operate? She didn't know how they function, how they tabulate votes, and how they report votes. On top of that, she didn't have the source code and didn't even perform any of the required functions to test the system. But that's just typical of our country right now. These officials gaslight everyone and declare how safe the election was without having the slightest knowledge regarding the very machines used to count the votes. It was a lie; it was a fraud that she committed on everyone in the State of Michigan and everyone in the country.

CHAPTER 15

With the help of Seth Keshel, who is regarded as one of the foremost intel patriots, Maryland joined a growing list of states that were looking into the integrity of their election systems across all counties. Files of data collected by the Maryland secretary of state's office showed that the last three presidential elections (2012, 2016, 2020) produced significant trends. In each of the four counties of focus, Anne Arundel, Carroll, Frederick, and Harford, these specific trends are crystal clear:

• In all four counties in the 2012 and 2016 elections, the Democratic vote increase remained marginal, ranging between 1% and 2% overall.

• Votes in 2020 for the Democratic Party in the counties examined showed an uptick, though this increase was not significant enough to alter the predicted result of the election.

The need for a full forensic audit of the 2020 election in Maryland has been highlighted in these findings, given the severity of the anomalies, and as we know, such incidents of mass inaccuracies in state election systems are not limited to just one state, but numerous. Multiple investigations were ongoing in several states, including Michigan, Georgia, and Arizona during 2021. The results of the primary elections in New York City also showed how these anomalies affected outcomes and the voters themselves.

In the New York City Democratic primary, which took place on June 22nd, 2021, voters were able to cast their ballot using ranked-choice voting. The results showed that Kathryn Garcia and Eric Adams were almost tied at the end of the day, with less than a 1% margin point for Adams.

Soon after, the New York Board of Elections revealed that it had mistakenly included 135,000 test ballots in its interim results. The results were later corrected. Every single candidate filed a lawsuit to have the votes counted again, and the results were later adjusted. It was revealed in the Associated Press that Adams led Garcia by 14,755 votes.

Chair of the Maryland Voter Integrity Group, Robyn Sachs, stated: "The unexplainable spikes in these four Maryland Counties are a call to action to chase down any inaccuracies and potential fraud that are eroding Americans' confidence in our electoral systems. The data we are seeing signals that now is the time to act to preserve the American birthright of free, fair, and transparent elections for all."

Many petitions were created once it became clear that fraud was very much a reality, and so Maryland Voter Integrity Group led the charge by launching its petition to audit the vote in Maryland in the 2020 presidential election, hoping that, like Arizona, the voters of Maryland would be enfranchised.

This initiative was part of the organization's goal to prevent voter fraud and inaccuracies in Maryland's voter rolls. Per the times and to receive as many signatures as possible, the petition could be signed digitally on the group's website, calling for a full forensic audit of Maryland's elections, hopefully clarifying anomalies discovered within Anne Arundel, Carroll, Frederick, and Harford counties in Maryland.

The operation, however, didn't stop there. After unearthing more civilian-sourced evidence regarding voter discrepancies, further mathematical analysis was conducted by a PhD candidate with an extensive cybersecurity and engineering background, who later proposed that a computer algorithm had affected the 2020 election in Maryland.

Using a combination of publicly available data and complex algorithms, Maryland was able to show a drop in a large number of votes during Election Day, coincidently around the same time other states stopped counting and sent people home for the night.

Within a 4-minute window, the vote count rose almost 200% compared to the total number of votes received before the anomaly, indicating that the votes had more than 100% greater percentage totals than the cumulative votes' totals before this drop, and those data anomalies continued after the drop, with the new vote totals maintaining Biden's lead, even though there were still votes to be counted.

Key findings raise concerns about the accuracy of Maryland's electoral process and underscore the need for a full forensic audit.

"There's a clause in the Maryland Constitution: Article 1, Section 7. 'The General Assembly shall pass Laws necessary for the preservation of the purity of Elections.' That is precisely what we are asking for in our petition as concerned Marylanders and American citizens," Chair of the Maryland Voter Integrity Group, Robyn Sachs said. "We will continue to stand up for free, fair, and transparent elections, and believe the full forensic audit is necessary to get to the bottom of the anomalies we have discovered so far and to restore public faith in our elections."

Seth Keshel discovered several odd trends in the voting patterns of some counties, which have been reliable for over a century. Vote counts for every state were published, which showed the counties with the most favorable trends in voter registrations.

It was estimated that there may have been over 128,000 votes for Biden that were more than the total number of votes in Maryland, a very likely sign of election fraud.

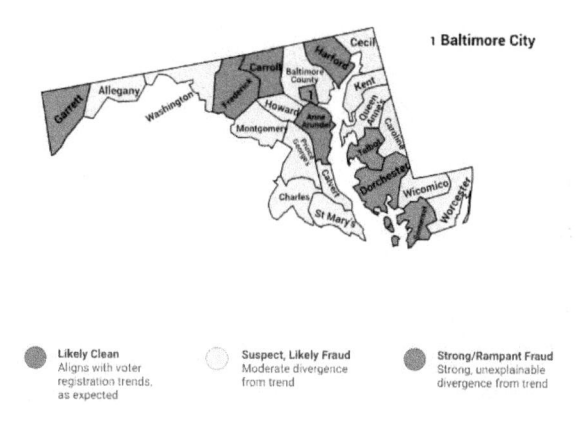

1 Baltimore City

Likely Clean
Aligns with voter registration trends, as expected

Suspect, Likely Fraud
Moderate divergence from trend

Strong/Rampant Fraud
Strong, unexplainable divergence from trend

Verified Voting has listed the locations of the voting equipment used in each county in the U.S. These are also listed in the databases of Verified Voting. The security features of the ballot marking equipment were different from those of the scanners and ballot boxes. Also, they require special equipment to be secure.

	Est Excess Votes (1000s)	Pop Growth Decade	2020 New RVs	2020 Registration Shift
ALLEGANY	1	-6%	892	7.2%
ANNE ARUNDEL	20	8%	28893	3.4%
BALTIMORE CITY	0	-6%	9156	0.4%
BALTIMORE CO.	15	3%	19414	0.2%
CALVERT	3	4%	5363	1.4%
CAROLINE	1	1%	1920	6.5%
CARROLL	8	1%	6153	1.1%
CECIL	3	2%	4596	6.0%
CHARLES	5	11%	10049	5.2%
DORCHESTER	0	-2%	1068	6.4%
FREDERICK	8	11%	22202	5.1%
GARRETT	0	-4%	827	5.4%
HARFORD	12	4%	13061	0.6%
HOWARD	5	14%	19208	7.0%
KENT	1	-4%	622	3.5%
MONTGOMERY	20	8%	19577	5.3%
PR. GEORGE'S	15	5%	31600	0.2%
QUEEN ANNE'S	2	5%	3206	2.3%
SOMERSET	0	-3%	754	7.8%
ST. MARY'S	2	8%	4807	1.0%
TALBOT	0	-2%	1524	2.5%
WASHINGTON	2	3%	5645	1.3%
WICOMICO	3	5%	4689	0.9%
WORCESTER	2	2%	2908	5.5%

According to experts, there is no way to fully secure a voting system or election system. As more sophisticated systems get added to them, the more they get, the more they become vulnerable to attack. As we've said before, the efficiency gains provided by machines are not reason enough to tolerate the loss of security, accountability, and transparency. Considering it was a state overwhelmingly favoring Biden, there is a startling amount of excess Dem votes, largely in Republican territory.

The primary takeaways from past inspections were that Baltimore City trended clean; however, that doesn't mean there wasn't any evidence of fraud, just a clean trend.

It should be noted that Keshel's estimates were based on the percentage of voters who were registered to each party (where it's possible to obtain this information) compared to the actual votes for each party. He examined these party trends over the last two decades, as well as population growth, which brought to light the strange and statistically unlikely outliers and anomalies that occurred in 2020.

At the time of inspection, Frederick County did seem to tend towards a more Democrat voting pool, as lead investigators noted that the figures presented the Democrats with an edge. Republicans are learning how the game is played after uncovering so much fraud, but the Democrats don't exactly cheat with variety. Let me tell you what I mean by this.

Even with a 77,000-vote increase, when you take Hartford County, for example, the vote increased for Democrats at a rate of 35% with no other correlation to the population of the registration group. Now this figure alone would suggest that there was substantial fraud for those figures to make any logical sense. Yet the trend just continues to worsen in favor of the Democrat's integrity. The first three slides of the Keshel report showed Frederick County, Anne Arundel County, and Hartford County, all with a voter increase of 35%. Now, I'm no logistician, but that doesn't sound right, surely. With all 3 of those counties being investigated by analysts, and all 3 of them having the same percentage of Democrat voter increase without any reliable explanation for the surge in voter turnout, where does the connection come from?

Although Hartford, like many other Maryland counties, is predominantly red, voters witnessed 63,000 legit votes for Joe Biden added to the total, supposedly. As an American citizen, seeing this happening in almost every state is completely sickening. We're talking about tens of thousands of votes being fabricated from nothing. What's even more concerning is that these machines aren't even registering additional people who are still living. Most of these fabricated votes came from the deceased, non-existent, illegal, or phantom voters.

Further canvassing occurred to ratify how many of the ballots were registered to living voters and which ones were completely unethical and fraudulent; ultimately though, the funds and the efforts to manifest an audit of Maryland and these key counties never materialized. Thousands of people made attempts to contact senators and delegates to make it happen, but like almost every instance of justice, the establishment crushed our chances.

It was believed that the citizens of Maryland could fund their audit with an initial investment of $150,000 for a forensic audit of Hartford County, which would have cost $2 per ballot, meaning a forensic audit, Arizona style, would have cost law-abiding citizens $300,000.

All the chairs of boards of elections and the Montgomery County chair don't necessarily care about the election audits because those boards aren't Republican-based. The majority of them are simply following what the legislature is ruling them to do, which is to turn a blind eye, look the other way, and forget about 2020.

The Board of Elections in Baltimore subsequently put out a rumor trying to denounce Seth's data, even though Seth used the data that they provided. The independent analysts used the actual votes, whereas the Board of Elections tried to bypass this discovery by publishing their findings, which only used the registration numbers, not even by county. So again, I know the story becomes more demoralizing the more you read, but this is what we're up against. It's not a fight against a few individuals. It's a systemic cold war between the ruling class and the working man. It's an intellectual battle to see who will throw in the towel first, and we can't let this defeat slide.

CHAPTER 16

The previous chapters detailed how we got here and how we might address it, but why did we get here? What motivated so many people to either be complicit or actively negligent in the perpetration of this illegal voting scheme? What sort of person would do this? What end goals did they have in mind? What was the purpose of the crime of the century?

I can think of several possibilities. One or all these potential motivations could be applied simultaneously. I will detail my thoughts on each of the following separately:
- Trump Derangement Syndrome
- COVID Lockdown Relief
- The Great Reset and Western Authoritarianism

Ever since Trump came on to the political scene, the media has lurched uncontrollably into a near frenzied state. Years of false Russia collusion stories artificially created racist headlines and prosecutorial misconduct amplified by the media's megaphone. One must wonder where all this came from. We have seen Republicans bashed before, but never to this extent - decades-old allegations of sexual conduct against Trump, contrasting with total disregard for Biden's bizarre behavior around children. Trump was impeached for a phone call with Ukraine; Biden took millions from Ukraine through his son and Burisma. A completely fabricated conspiracy around Trump and Russia, but there was a real conspiracy involving Clinton and the Russian Dossier. There was major coverage of a made-up story regarding Trump statements to veterans, but complete censorship of Hunter Biden's laptops proving the influence peddling in Ukraine. None of the latter stories made anywhere near as much coverage time as the former ones.

What caused this apparent delusion or derangement? What made the left hate Donald Trump to the extreme? While the answer does not matter for the sake of this chapter, I can posit a few theories.

Was it his brash and often in-your-face demeanor towards the press? He often refers to "fake news" as the "enemy of the people." Did that anger the media so much that they turned on him as the enemy? And then like "sheeple," did the average liberal followed suit with the media programming?

Perhaps it was his anti-establishment message? As this book illustrates, nearly every bureaucratic institution was weaponized against Trump. Did the Times magazine's "cabal" simply fear for their wealth and power, and, as a result, turn Big Tech, Big Media, Big Intelligence, and Big Government against Trump? Possibly . . .

Maybe it was the let-down that was Hillary Clinton? Many people were excited about the first woman president. Just no one wanted Hillary to be the first woman president . . .

Regardless of the reason, many people had a serious mental breakdown when Trump became president. He was a "racist" or a "fascist" or "war-hungry" or "incompetent" – however, the irony is that all of the things they accuse Trump of, are exactly what Biden embodies. Remember when Biden said, "If you don't vote for me, you ain't black?" Or how about when Biden shut down energy production in the USA, just to give Russia more leverage? Or perhaps you remember Biden's fascist obsession with locking up political dissidents, censoring information, and mandating unwanted medical procedures?

I suppose that it is possible that people, due to media derangement, simply felt it was OK to game the electoral system. Many executives from Google to the New York Times were heard saying, "no matter what it takes, as long as we stop him [Trump]." These people were willing to sacrifice democracy to achieve their goals in the name of **their** version of "democracy." While this is probably part of the reason for the coup, I think there is more to it than that.

Enter COVID. There was no greater distinction between the two Americas than red states and blue states during the COVID lockdown. In red states, there never really was a lockdown. Schools were open, businesses were bustling, the vulnerable were protected, and life went on as normal. blue states resembled some Soviet-style dictatorship: parks and playgrounds with chains over basketball hoops, sand poured into skateboarding arenas, grocery stores closed except for drive-thru only, small businesses destroyed, vaccine passports and Nazi-style "show me your papers" policies, useless masks mandated to walk outside, Gestapo police tactics arresting priests who dared to hold services, while Anti-Fa rioters outside were celebrated, etc.

The Biden victory ensured a fresh economic surge with a welfare package that redistributed $1.9 trillion from the majority of red states to the rest of the country. The American Rescue Plan was a great success in this regard, as it furthered the state-level corruption and totalitarian lockdown measures for the foreseeable future, and as businesses went under and people failed to pay for necessities without a government handout, the Dems looked the other way, racking it up as just another inconvenience that didn't require any real attention.

The COVID lockdowns destroyed blue state economies. And they wanted, no, they **needed**, a federal bail-out to survive. Trump and the Republicans were not going to give them that bailout for their misguided COVID policies. It was in these blue states' interests to break their own rules, change election protocols illegally, mass-send unsolicited mail-in ballots, remove signature requirements, and force out Republican poll monitors to steal the election. They wanted their bail-out money which, ultimately, they got, as part of Joe Biden's COVID relief package of $1.9 trillion. But could there be something even more nefarious than just simple desperation for money after failed COVID policies and shrinking state treasuries at foot?

The third motive I believe to be behind the steal is something far more sinister, yet growing in popularity amongst everyday citizens. For many months now, the public has been theorizing as to what COVID, the lockdowns, and the vaccines were subversively doing, all without looking at the people sustaining the protocols. The underlying commonality is that these incumbents all derive from the same school of thought. The pandemic has been a guise, perpetuated by known and unknown charlatans, individuals who are politically and financially interlinked and completely backed by a single organization.

The organization in question is the World Economic Forum, its Great Reset plan, and its Young Global Leaders initiative: an independent non-profit organization managed from the neutrality of Geneva, under the direction of the Swiss Government. The development was launched by Klaus Schwab in 2004, where it was to be overseen by a board of 12 political and industry leaders, tasked with quashing the world's greatest problems. Members range from the likes of Rania Al Abdullah (Queen Consort of Jordan) and Marissa Mayer (CEO of Yahoo) to Jimmy Donal Wales (Co-founder of Wikipedia) and Leonardo DiCaprio.

The organization plans to drive global development and alter the relationship between public and private domains (communism), further facilitating globalism and transhumanism by sponsoring the careers of its members. Alumni of the WEF program have risen to power across the world, all within the same 20-year period. Because billionaires pushed for lockdowns due to a virus that has an IFR that is on par with the flu for most age groups, the greatest transfer of wealth in human history from the middle class to the elite quietly occurred as the masses focused on a virus that they were told was of paramount importance.

The newly formed totalitarian state of New Zealand is currently battling the yoke of a governing body spearheaded by Jacinda Ardern (Prime Minister of New Zealand), who received a generous Freemason scholarship that put her through university at the behest of Klaus Schwab. She was also the president of the International Union of Socialist Youth in the late 2000s, an era she spent propagating communist conventions in her speeches. Just last month, Ardern announced the introduction of vaccine passports, which are set to be used to regulate civil freedoms across the nation.

Ardern is just one of the numerous leaders indebted to the Klaus Schwab school of COVID dictators, collectively setting the precedent for an impending cultural schism and economic reset. The unknown alliance of corporate and political leaders deployed the pandemic to crash national economies, using the alumni of Young Global Leaders as their advertising campaign to reassure the public.

New Zealand is not alone. Part of the WEF's plan is to encourage censorship of dissident information, imprison non-like-minded individuals, reduce the opportunity for individuals to own property, and transfer that wealth into the hands of billionaire conglomerates. They want to force medical procedures on the unwilling and destroy religion to replace it with neo-liberalism, "climate change" (whatever that is), and anti-population directives designed to make the planet more "liveable." Have you seen what Australia has been doing to its citizens? How about the doctors in America that have been silenced, the January 6th gulag, the truckers in Canada, or the nurses and soldiers fired for not taking an experimental gene therapy, never provided their constitutional right to freedom of religious belief? This is the rise of Western fascism playing out right in front of us.

Other notable names on the WEF's roster are Emmanuel Macron, the President of France; Sebastian Kurz, who was until recently the Chancellor of Austria; Viktor Orban, Prime Minister of Hungary; and Jean-Claude Juncker, former Prime Minister of Luxembourg and President of the European Commission. Almost 190 world governments used the same illogical policies when dealing with the pandemic, cohesively strangling their constituents with lockdowns, mask mandates, mandatory vaccines, and vaccine passports. Why is this?

Given the growing discontent with the anti-COVID measures put into practice by the school's graduates who are now national leaders, many believe is possible that these people were selected due to their willingness to do whatever they are told, and that they are being set up to fail so that the subsequent backlash can be exploited to justify the creation of a new global form of government. Indeed, politicians with unique personalities and strong, original views have become rarer, and the distinguishing characteristics of the national leaders of the past 30 years have been their meekness and adherence to a strict globalist line dictated from above. This has been especially evident in most countries' response to the pandemic, where politicians who knew nothing about viruses two years ago suddenly proclaimed that COVID was a severe health crisis that justified locking people up in their homes, shutting down their businesses, and wrecking entire economies.

Graduates from the Young Global Leaders school and Global Leaders for Tomorrow find themselves very well-situated given that they then have access to the WEF's network of contacts. The WEF's current Board of Trustees includes such luminaries as

Christine Lagarde, former Managing Director of the International Monetary Fund; current President of the European Central Bank, Queen Rania of Jordan, who has been ranked by Forbes as one of the 100 most powerful women in the world; and Larry Fink, CEO of BlackRock. the largest investment management corporation internationally, which handles approximately $9 trillion in assets annually. By tracing the connections between the school's graduates, you can see that they continue to rely on each other for support for their initiatives, long after they participated in the Global Leaders programs.

Part of the reason we will never see the media, mainstream doctors, government, or any of the aforementioned people tell the truth is because they're all one organization, dedicated to installing a worldwide digital currency under draconian measures (similar to the Chinese Social Credit System), whereby people have very little freedoms beyond what is granted by the Credit Pass (Vaccine Passport).

They're playing this to the end no matter what happens long-term or short-term. They'll never concede the narrative. For this reason, they won't even acknowledge the billions of people who are already naturally immune, let alone tell the truth about the efficacy of masks and lockdowns, and why countries are destroying their economies for a virus that 99.9% recover from. Everyone knows the pharmaceutical industry controls governments, corporations influence governments, and they're often all the same, and many of the talking heads are in the pocket. This is not a mind-blowing take. But if faith in America's institutions completely dies, everything with crumble. Letting them occupy arguably the foremost institution in the free world will affect us all if it isn't met with vigor and patriotism.

So, what can we do about all of this? Short of armed revolution (which appears more likely day after day), what possibilities do we have to secure election integrity and transparency? There are a few options; in every state, we must demand:

- Voter identification for in-person voting (for those claiming this disproportionately affects the disadvantaged, have paid-for delivery services to provide identification)
- Serial, identification, or social security numbers on all absentee and mail-in ballots
- Signature verification required on all ballots
- No more unsolicited mailed ballots, they must be requested with a reason defined by the state's legislatures
- State and/or federal criminalization of ignoring a state's constitution and/or existing election-related legislation by an executive or judicial power within that state held by an opposing party
- That states must pass legislation that makes audits **mandatory** after every major election (why not?)
- Records of ballot images for 22 months, as required by federal law – if a state does not comply, those in charge must be held accountable by federal law, with charges including imprisonment
- Enforce poll monitoring requirements at state, local, and federal level – no ballot may be counted unless observed by both parties
- Avoidance of electronic machines – encourage via state purchasing power the culmination of many different vote tabulation technologies – never again may one company determine the outcome of an election (This should be done redundantly. Vote twice, on two different machines, and combine them in the consolidated results tabulation. Why not?)
- The end of ballot harvesting in every state- where applicable, provide video and cellular tracking of those engaging in ballot harvestingCriminalization on a federal level of coercing the elderly, infirm, or mentally disabled, to be able to fill out a ballot at the coercion of another and absolute enforcement this timeNetwork(s) of social media

designed to report infractions that are not subject to Silicon Valley minions that prefer one political affiliation over another.
- That presence at polling stations be showed, without being intimidated – your vote counts as much as their fake votes (Build coalitions locally, assemble, and inspect the votes. Do not allow people in power to rob you of your rights to vote, and ensure your representatives are allowed to be involved and inspect the votes coming in.)
- Approach towards blockchain technology, coupled with middleware encryption designed to prevent hijacking between transit points (a must!)
- Enforcement of the Truth in Broadcasting Act of 2005 – no longer can we simply accept opinion-based pundit programming
- Finally, **holding everyone accountable** - those that say, "2020 is over, whatever," miss the point; it will happen again, over and over; those responsible must be held accountable.

I bid you good fortune in the coming years, **patriots**. I don't know how things will pan out, but if we have community, solidarity, integrity, and resolve, nothing can destroy our spirit.

Until next time, stay safe, be vigilant . . .
And fight for freedom.

-D. A.

COUP SOURCES

DISCLAIMER: THIS IS A NON-EXHAUSTIVE LIST. SOME OF THESE LINKS MAY HAVE BEEN CENSORED DURING THE TIME OF PUBLISHING

- https://www.readingeagle.com/pa-gop-lawmaker-mastriano-doubles-down-on-election-audit-requests-meeting-with-president-biden/article_da029166-e41d-11eb-9a08-d3b3f83cf084.html
- https://www.ajc.com/politics/some-ballots-initially-double-counted-in-fulton-before-recount/GY4FTEEI6REIJN3SDKIDNIOYV4/
- https://www.kvue.com/article/news/verify/texas-voter-fraud-cases-verify/269-205e72be-17a1-4c34-8156-8321ff1ddd78
- https://www.nbc4i.com/news/your-local-election-hq/ohio-identifies-13-possible-cases-of-voterfraud-in-2020-election/
- https://www.heritage.org/voterfraud
- https://mpra.ub.uni-muenchen.de/105118/3/MPRA_paper_105118.pdf
- https://papers.ssrn.com/sol3/Papers.cfm?abstract_id=3666259
- https://papers.ssrn.com/sol3/papers.cfm?abstract_id=3849068
- https://repository.law.umich.edu/cgi/viewcontent.cgi?article=1036&context=librarian
- https://www.sciencedirect.com/science/article/pii/S026137942030041X

- https://www.researchgate.net/profile/Savva-Shanaev/publication/347606599_Detecting_Anomalies_in_the_2020_US_Presidential_Election_Votes_with_Benford%27s_Law/links/5fe4990692851c13feb8ffac/Detecting-Anomalies-in-the-2020-US- Presidential-Election-Votes-with-Benfords-Law.pdf
- https://arxiv.org/pdf/2011.13015
- https://academiccommons.columbia.edu/doi/10.7916/D85147P9/download
- https://www.gregpalast.com/wp-content/uploads/OnePersonOneVote.pdf
- https://www.d11.org/cms/lib/CO02201641/Centricity/Domain/3824/SSRN-id3756988.pdf
- https://www.hoover.org/sites/default/files/research/docs/comment_voterfraud_grimmer_garro_egg ers.pdf
- https://arxiv.org/pdf/2011.13015
- https://www.researchgate.net/profile/Andre-E- Vellwock/publication/344164702_Is_COVID- 19_data_reliable_A_statistical_analysis_with_Benford's_Law/links/5f64b510458515b7cf3c5925/Is-COVID-19-data-reliable-A-statistical-analysis-with- Benfords-Law.pdf
- https://hereistheevidence.com/
- https://challengesweface.org/fraud-analyst-finds-average-of-2-to-3-percent- shift-for-biden-in-counties-that-used-dominion/
- https://ideasanddata.wordpress.com/2020/11/10/evidence-of-voter-fraud-inthe-2020-us-presidential-election/
- https://votepatternanalysis.substack.com/p/voting-anomalies-2020
- https://www.theepochtimes.com/statistical-anomalies-in-biden-votes- analyses-indicate_3570518.html
- https://billmoyers.com/story/fabricated-ballots-dead-voters-and-other- phantom-fears-from-trump-supporters-at-georgia-presidential-audit/

- https://www.goodmorningliberty.us/post/yes-there-were-statistical-anomalies-on-election-day-now-what
- https://www.tampabay.com/news/military/2020/11/01/floridas-military-mail-in- vote-may-play-critical-role-in-2020-election/
- https://voterga.org/wp-content/uploads/2021/07/Zero-trump-tally-sheets.pdf
- https://voterga.org/
- https://www.youtube.com/watch?v=VD7qrjialwg&ab_channel=GarlandFavorito
- https://www.youtube.com/watch?v=Oh5j7s1H7ek&ab_channel=DonaldJTrump
- https://ballotpedia.org/Presidential_election_in_Georgia,_2020
- https://rumble.com/vjxs84-theres-proof-of-voter-fraud-in-fulton-county-georgia.html
- https://rumble.com/vjvqva-tucker-airs-hard-evidence-of-voter-fraud-in-georgia-and-breaks-the-internet.html
- https://rumble.com/vjssnp-scanned-ballots-images-proof-of-voter-fraud.html
- https://rumble.com/vlokd6-garland-favorito-voterga-suing-to-ban-use-of-barcodes-on-ballots-in-ga.-ele.html
- https://www.youtube.com/watch?v=oDDcqXuWnTg&ab_channel=Sivaady
- https://voterga.org/wp-content/uploads/2021/06/lindell-complaint-dominion-6421.pdf
- https://voterga.org/wp-content/uploads/2021/06/curling-v-raffensperger-rulling-101120.pdf
- https://rumble.com/vbicwr-pennsylvania-bombshell.-paul-kengor-with-sebastian-gorka-on-america-first.html
- https://rumble.com/vdotgn-pennsylvania-2020-election-fraud-allegations.html
- https://www.bitchute.com/video/mspk1OWTlWnp/
- https://www.bitchute.com/video/1cjxl5gGfgpV/
- https://www.bitchute.com/video/NOwjdugkXnxP/

- https://www.bitchute.com/video/313MGivResuv/
- https://www.bitchute.com/video/A3IlPJzx323n/
- https://www.bitchute.com/video/MIsmcLnRuIZv/
- https://www.bitchute.com/video/A3IlPJzx323n/
- https://rumble.com/vjrib5-pennsylvania-poll-watcher-47-usb-cards-missing-100k-ballots-in-question.html
- https://rumble.com/vjrhmn-pennsylvania-423166-votes-subtracted-from-trump.html
- https://rumble.com/vbgsob-live-on-cnn-trumps-vote-total-drops-by-19958-at-the-exact-same-time-biden-g.html
- https://rumble.com/vh1ufp-irrefutable-proof-2020-presidential-election-fraud.html
- https://www.thegatewaypundit.com/2021/07/bombshell-seth-keshel-trump-won-pennsylvania-6-8-video/
- https://www.thegatewaypundit.com/2021/08/seth-keshel-releases-analysis-five-pennsylvania-counties-enough-fraudulent-ballots-flip-state-trump/
- http://www.repdiamond.com/News/18754/Latest-News/PA-Lawmakers-Numbers-Don%E2%80%99t-Add-Up,-Certification-of-Presidential-Results-Premature-and-In-Error
- https://www.legis.state.pa.us/cfdocs/legis/LI/consCheck.

CPSIA information can be obtained
at www.ICGtesting.com
Printed in the USA
BVHW032233090722
641765BV00013B/474